THE

Aubreigh Wyatt

STORY

HEATHER WYATT

Identifiers:
979-8-9997898-0-8 paperback
979-8-9997898-1-5 ebook

Printed in the United States of America

This is a work of nonfiction. Some of the names, events, and experiences are presented to the best of the author's memory. In some cases, identifying details have been changed to protect the privacy of individuals.

Cover design by Marie Stirk.

Disclaimer: This book does not offer professional medical or therapeutic advice. The events described in this book are from my perspective and interpretation.

To: Aubreigh

Love, Mom

CONTENTS

1

May in Mississippi doesn't ease you into summer. It hits you like a brick wall of humidity. The air was thick and sticky by mid-morning, the kind that makes your hair frizz and your skin feel permanently damp. But inside our home, it wasn't the heat that made things feel heavy; it was worry.

Ryker, my five-year-old son, had been hospitalized for five days following a boating trip that led to a serious infection. It was intense and scary. But we stayed strong. His dad, Dexter, his stepmom, Kelly, and I were there every step of the way. All three of us stayed every night during the hospital stay. I still don't know if that was allowed. Regardless, none of us was leaving our baby. We have a fabulous co-parenting relationship, and during those days, we were a team.

Being away from home at night was especially hard. As a mom to three children, and being pulled away from two of them—my daughters, Taylor and Aubreigh—felt unnatural. Taylor, my oldest, was nearly 15 at the time, and wise beyond her years, with a fierce heart and the most compassionate soul. And then there's Aubreigh, my middle child, newly 13, sunshine and spark all wrapped into one. It didn't feel right not tucking them in, not hearing the late-night chatter or laughter echoing down the hallway. I missed their hugs, their presence, the rhythm of our little home.

Every afternoon after school, Aubreigh and Taylor would come to visit Ryker. That tiny hospital room transformed the moment they walked in. It was suddenly a little home away from home. It was full of laughter, pranks, and pure chaos in the best way. We took turns cuddling Ryker, stealing the rare decent food off the trays, and cracking jokes that had the nurses laughing, too.

The staff didn't just tolerate us; they joined in. Nurses would peek their heads in just to hear what we were laughing about this time and chuckle as they checked vitals. There was love in that room, family, unity. Even amidst the worry, we created joy.

Taylor and Aubreigh, even when they weren't physically there, would text constantly. "How's Ryker today?" "Is he eating anything?" "Tell him I love him!" They wanted updates and photos and to be part of it all, even in the moments they couldn't be. One day after school, Aubreigh texted, "Are we still going to the concert?" I didn't know. I wanted to say yes, but everything was uncertain.

The Megan Moroney concert had already been on the calendar. We weren't even sure we'd make it.

By May 17th, Ryker was still in the hospital. His catheter had finally been removed, but we weren't allowed to go home until he could urinate on his own. The concert was only two days away, and the clock was ticking. We were starting to get nervous. Regardless, we would be fine as long as Ryker was better.

We tried everything that day: water, juice, Sprite. He drank and drank, and we waited. We cheered him on, encouraged him, and sang silly songs like "Peepee in the Potty," even though what we were really rooting for was a hospital-issued handheld urinal. Nothing.

By 7:00 p.m., we had given up hope of going home that night. We figured we'd try again tomorrow.

And then, at 7:45, Ryker perked up and said, "I gotta go."

He was hesitant, nervous, but we all jumped up like a cheer squad. We clapped, chanted, encouraged him, and then...

Finally, he did it.

He peed in that dang urinal!

Ryker and I ran down the hospital hallway with his gown flapping open in the back, wind blowing as we laughed and screamed, holding up that pee-filled urinal like it was a gold medal. Booty out and all.

Unbothered!

We ran to the nurses' station, shouting and laughing, proud as could be. My baby was healed! My baby was better.

I thought we'd still have to wait until morning for discharge now, as it was already 7:54 p.m.

But the doctors and nurses moved fast. The team sprang into action, and just like that, we were discharged. Home again. Back with my baby girls. All my kiddos under one roof, happy, and healthy. My mama heart was ecstatic.

Concert was a go.

But we hadn't had time to shop. Not even a little. We had been in the hospital right up until the night of the 17th, and the next day was a Thursday. We were tired, behind, and totally unprepared. So on May 18th, we scrambled. We dug through closets and texted friends looking for cowgirl boots in every size. It was all thrown together at the last-minute—mismatched and unplanned.

And it turned out perfect.

That Friday, May 19th, 2023, we were a mess. I was home from the hospital, and everything was chaos. There were laundry piles everywhere, dishes piled up, and school bags tossed across the floor. Everyone had school that morning, which threw our whole rhythm off. By the time we were all home and scrambling to get ready, we were already running behind. It was sticky-hot outside, the sun blazing with that humid Mississippi glare.

We all crammed into the car in our boots.

Yep. Boots in May.

And we headed toward the Mississippi Coast Coliseum. Traffic was a nightmare. I'm talking full brake-to-brake gridlock. I kept checking the time, heart pounding, knowing that Megan Moroney was *the opener*, not the headliner. That was our girl. We weren't going for anyone else.

By the time we found parking, we were in a dead sprint. Cowboy boots thudding across pavement, heat rising in visible waves off the blacktop. We rushed into the venue, not even bothering to find our cheap nosebleed seats that I had purchased. And somehow, miraculously, an entire section down near the stage was open. Nobody was there. So we took the chance. I told the girls, "If someone comes, we'll move. But for now, let's enjoy this." I know, I know, *mom fail*. Wrong seats, wrong section. But in true laid-back, winging-it fashion, we were already laughing about it as we moved.

We missed the first few lines of her opening song, but we were there. The music was loud, the crowd buzzing, and we danced like idiots. We were laughing, screaming, completely out of pitch, sounding more like squawking birds than concert-goers. But it didn't matter. Taylor and Aubreigh had their phones out, taking selfies, making videos, sending Snapchats, and capturing every wild moment. I watched them as much as I watched the stage, completely mesmerized. As much as I loved the music and loved being there, what truly warmed my heart was seeing my girls soak it all in. It was their first concert, and they were glowing.

I didn't have a mother growing up, or get to experience things like this, so giving my girls these kinds of experiences meant everything to me. It probably healed a part of my own childhood I didn't even know was still tender. Just watching these two beautiful people that I created, laughing, singing, and living so fully, filled me with so much love and admiration. It was pure joy.

Aubreigh looked like an angel. She wore a beautiful white dress, flowy and fun, her favorite. Her long blonde hair was curled into soft beach waves, and on her feet were her blue glitter cowgirl boots. Her lashes, as always, were flawless; she never went anywhere without making sure they were just right. Taylor wore the same dress, but in a fresh, grassy green, with long brown hair curled into the same beach waves and brown cowgirl boots. I had on a black romper dress and white boots, and yes, my hair was curled too. Beach waves for all of us. Our signature look.

We were a trio of sparkle and southern sass, and we soaked in every second.

I watched my girls twirl and laugh like nothing bad had ever happened to either of them before. With every giggle I heard come out of Aubreigh's mouth, I imagined all the negative and nasty encounters from that year evaporating in the summer heat. I did what I could to push it out of my mind, but a mother always remembers.

It had only been two months since the latest burst of toxicity she had to endure at school around a particular cruel group of girls. It was always the same girls.

Aubreigh had been dealing with bullying for years, since fifth grade. Aubreigh had always been well-liked by most in that way that made her a target. She was pretty, popular, had a big personality, and worst of all, to some kids, she was kind. Not fake-nice. Not people-pleasing. Genuinely kind.

And they hated her for it. And for years, tormented her.

She wasn't just left out of group chats; she received a cold shoulder in the hallway, and friends who suddenly weren't friends anymore.

But over time, the cruelty sharpened. Girls who once invited her for sleepovers were now whispering behind her back. One day, they'd post pictures together, and the next, she'd be completely shut out.

They'd be her best friend for one week, laughing in the hallway, taking selfies together, hanging out at school events, and hanging out on FaceTime. Then, like flipping a switch, the next, they were whispering behind her back, they'd be turning others against her, starting group chats without her and about her, spreading rumors, mocking her appearance, and mocking her on social media, even encouraging her to self-harm.

In March of 2023, Aubreigh reported being sexually assaulted at a school sports event.

When it first happened, Aubreigh was just twelve years old. A seventh grader.

A boy at school had crossed a line. She was scared, unsure, but brave enough to speak. She said she didn't want to be called a snitch, but she also said, 'What he did is bad, and either way, he should be in trouble.'

She had been sexually assaulted by a classmate. Someone she knew. Someone the school knew. A boy who should never have been allowed near her again.

But when she found the courage to speak up, the very people who were supposed to protect her—the adults, the school administrators, the system—turned their backs.

We filed a report immediately, following the proper channels. I was clear in my boundaries: **no one was to question her without an adult present.** I told them firmly that *she is a child*. She deserves to be protected. Supported. Heard. I told the school what she had shared. She also gave her statement, and I gave clear, firm instructions: Do not question her without me.

But they didn't listen.

The principal pulled her in alone. My 12-year-old daughter, fresh off the most terrifying thing she'd ever shared, was sat down by a man in power and made to relive it. No mom. No advocate. No safety. She was alone. She was scared. And they used that fear against her.

And then came the emotional manipulation. They told her people wouldn't believe her. That she would ruin his life. That she'd have to tell her story over and over, to rooms full of strangers. They warned her that if she went forward, she would "ruin his life." That his family didn't believe her. They told her it would be hard. And they made it harder.

At school, kids started choosing sides. Literal sides. There was 'Team him' and 'Team Aubreigh.' Someone posted online, 'It's really not that deep... she could've stopped him while he was doing it.'

As if her trauma were a game and gossip.

She came home frantic one afternoon, really upset. Her voice cracked, trembling, as she whispered through tears, "I'm scared, Momma... everybody is gonna believe him over me... I can't do this."

I held her in my arms and kissed the top of her head. I wanted to protect her forever, while tearing down the walls of that school and scolding all those kids involved. But all I could do was remind her again and again that she wasn't alone.

"Honey, I'll do whatever you want me to do. But you can do this, Aubs. I got you," I calmly said back to her. "There are cameras at the stadium where he did it, and the school will discipline him."

That's what I believed. I believed the school would support us. I trusted the school representative I spoke to when I reported the incident. I was told the school would contact authorities, and I didn't need to. But in reality, nobody at her school supported her. Even her close friends backed off a bit because it was so intense at school. Her peers bullied her emotionally and psychologically until she began to doubt herself.

She was confused, shaken, unsure. She told me what they said. And I could see it sinking into her skin like poison. I watched her bright light go out as she told me that *they* made her feel like *she* had done something wrong.

Not him. *Her.*

My skin felt like it was on fire as I held her and kissed the top of her head. I reassured her that she was right and he was wrong. But the pain wasn't just in the assault itself; it was in the silencing that followed. My little girl was led to believe that her voice didn't matter. She was sent a message from adults around her that made her believe to her core that she didn't matter, her experience wasn't important, and she needed to pretend trauma that happened to her was all in her head.

A few days later, she withdrew the complaint. Not because it didn't happen. But because they wore her down. She hated being at school and just wanted to move on, take the spotlight off of her, and maybe people would forget it.

Aubreigh—who was already fragile, was already trying to hold her head up from being bullied by others for years—just stopped talking about it altogether.

She buried it. Not because it didn't hurt, but because it hurt *too much*.

I know she told herself it was possible to move on. She wanted to let it go, not because it didn't matter, but because it was breaking her. 'I don't want to talk about it anymore,' she told me. 'I just want to move on.'

I know she tried to survive. But how do you survive in a place where you're reminded every day that your safety, your story, and your pain don't matter?

She was tired. Of being brave. Of being blamed. Of trying to hold up a truth no one wanted to carry with her.

As a mother, every instinct in me screamed to fight. To push. To march down to that school and demand justice until they had no choice but to listen. I wanted to carry her pain, to shoulder it for her so she wouldn't have to. But I also knew I couldn't force her to keep reliving it. She was twelve. Twelve. Still a little girl, trying to hold herself together in a world that was already breaking her spirit. She had been questioned alone, made to feel responsible for what had been done to her, bullied by kids and adults alike into thinking she'd ruined someone's life just for telling the truth. I could see the weight it was taking on her. And so as much as it gutted me, I let her withdraw her complaint. Not because I believed it was the right thing, but because I knew *she* couldn't carry it anymore. I chose my daughter's peace over the fight.

The damage was already done. Not because of my baby girl, but because of the girls she went to school with.

Weeks later, one of those girls slapped Aubreigh in the face at school. I reported it. And the only thing the school did was remove the girl from a sports team. And then that girl had the nerve to text Aubreigh.

I wanted to shake off so many years of pain, trauma, and anxiety that night. We told ourselves it was nearly summer. We could have a break from her classmates, who never treated her right. But that particular school year, seventh grade, did something different to Aubreigh.

It changed her. Maybe even broke her.

And that night, at our first concert together, I was watching my daughters shine so bright nobody would have ever known anything awful had ever happened to either of them. Or in four months, one of them would decide to leave Earth on her terms.

I jumped around with my girls and shook off all the toxic crap from Aubreigh's seventh-grade year right alongside her. And when Megan finished her part of the set, we rushed outside to the balcony to take pictures. Something we would've done before the show, but since we were late and barely made it in time to catch her songs, we didn't want to miss a second of it. So we waited until after her set, and then we ran out to capture the moment.

The sun was starting to set, and the sky behind the Coliseum was streaked with soft pinks and warm gold, something that would later mean so much more to me. We laughed and posed and spun in circles in our boots, still breathless from the songs we had just belted at the top of our lungs.

It was one of those moments you bottle up and wish you could freeze. After pictures and water breaks, we went back inside. We stayed for the next act, too, still giddy and in that rush. But by then, we were just riding the wave. Eventually, we decided to beat the crowd and head out early.

Outside, Taylor kicked off her boots and skipped barefoot across the concrete in the parking lot, her socks turning black from the pavement. We laughed until we couldn't breathe. We couldn't find the car, and when I tried to beep the fob, the battery was dead. So we wandered the lot, half-lost, half-laughing.

When we finally found the car, we blasted Megan Moroney's album all the way home, windows down, voices hoarse. That night didn't feel special because it was a concert. It felt special because it was effortless joy, the kind you don't realize is rare until later.

10

June came and went with the usual mix of beach days and birthdays. We celebrated Taylor turning 15 with a beach trip to Florida! It was all sunscreen, laughter, and salt-sticky hair. The heat in June was no joke, high 90s most days, the kind where even the breeze felt warm. But the days were full. The girls had sleepovers, hung out with friends, went on boat trips, and saw movies. It was everything summer is supposed to be.

Then came July.

Aubreigh had been counting down the days until her first overnight and *out-of-state* youth trip. It was to M28 Camp in Lake Junaluska, North Carolina, July 3rd through 6th. We had gone shopping together to get her all the little things she needed. Travel-size everything, cute camp outfits, and a new water bottle. She was giddy. Nervous, but giddy. I was a nervous wreck to have her so far away, and for so long; it was her first real trip like this without family.

She bonded with other students over their love for God. They sang worship songs, participated in small-group devotionals, played volleyball, and shared their testimonies late into the night. They went whitewater rafting and paddle boarding and spent quiet time by the lake reflecting and praying. It was everything a youth retreat should be—fun, faith-filled, and unforgettable.

Towards the end of camp, she messaged me: "Mom. This is life-changing."

And then: "I'm going to be saved again."

She'd been baptized once before, at eight. But this time, she said it felt different. I was thrilled for her! I was sad I wasn't going to be there to witness her get rebaptized, but I knew she was in great hands. This time, she *understood*. It wasn't required, but in her heart, she needed to make that step. And she did.

She came home beaming with joy.

Not in a fake, surface way. In a deep, real way. Like she knew something different about the world and herself.

July was full of excitement.

Since Aubreigh was coming back from camp the day of Ryker's 6th birthday, we waited and celebrated on July 8th at a trampoline jump park. She joined in on all the fun, jumping, laughing, and running around with all of Ryker's little friends. She was always the best big sister. Fun and playful, but nurturing like a mama. We used to joke that she was his second mama.

After that, we went right into back-to-school chaos. New shoes. A new backpack. She wanted *Lululemon everything*, girly, trendy, all about the latest styles. She tried on outfits, asked my opinion a hundred times, and made TikToks in her room. She was *so* excited.

We spent days out on an island off the coast of Mississippi, just enjoying life and each other. At night, sometimes Aubreigh would help me prep for my new classroom. We'd sit side-by-side on the couch watching our favorite TV shows, stapling papers, and punching holes in paper and worksheets that I'd use in my classroom starting in the fall.

During the days, she'd come with me and help me decorate my new classroom.

Aubreigh was happy. She was loved. She was supported. She was silly and vibrant and bubbly. She was the girl next door. She laughed and danced and sent streaks on Snapchat. She loved hard and forgave easily.

She was ours.

And in the middle of it all, we had no idea of the storm that was coming.

2

AUGUST 4TH, 2023, WAS THE FIRST DAY OF EIGHTH GRADE.
Aubreigh stood in front of the mirror that morning wearing a light pink V-neck shirt, ripped jeans, and a pair of white sandals. Her long blonde hair was curled into loose waves, her go-to beachy look. Her lashes were, of course, flawless. She wouldn't leave the house until they were.

She looked beautiful. She *was* beautiful.

Nervous but excited. Hopeful.

I was dressed and ready for work, teaching 3rd grade that year, and needed to leave early. I wore a black top and white skinny jeans. Yes, skinny jeans—still holding on, even if Gen Z had declared them dead.

Ryker was bouncing around the house, dressed up for his first day of 1st grade in a white shirt that had his name spelled out in crayon letters, paired with gray shorts and gray tennis shoes. Taylor was heading into 10th grade, wearing a black blouse, light-wash jeans, and white tennis shoes. And like the typical mom in me, I was forcing those cliché first-day-of-school pictures, lining them up in front of the door, making them smile just one more time, smile big! Eye rolls and giddy laughter. I didn't want to forget a thing.

There was excitement. Nerves. But everyone looked good. Everyone was ready.

This was a fresh start. New year. New grade. But underneath all the usual back-to-school chaos, I could feel it: that little coil of dread twisting in my stomach. And that dread was around Aubreigh's class-mates. It was exhausting to keep up with who was "in" and who was "out." And Aubreigh? She always seemed to be right on the edge of both.

Some of them told her she wasn't enough. Some said she was *too much.* Some did both. Somebody shamed her, some called her a bitch, a slut. Some of them told her she was too sensitive, too dramatic, too emotional.

It was never-ending. I remember having long conversations with the girl's parents about things I didn't ever expect to have to talk about.

Back in 2020, Aubreigh was at a sleepover with two other girls, and her world was shaken in a way no child should ever face. While Aubreigh was changing, one of those girls took photos of Aubreigh's bare naked body and video. And then those two girls threatened to post the video and photos on social media. She was 10 years old at the time and absolutely distraught over the situation. What should have been a night of giggles and popcorn turned into a nightmare of embarrassment, threats, and shame.

As soon as I heard about it, I was on the phone with parents and assured discipline was being taken and that the footage was deleted.

And those two girls got into Aubreigh's head so badly, over the years, it just wore her down. It wasn't always loud or obvious. Sometimes it was whispers, side glances, or messages dropped into group chats late at night. Sometimes it was accusations; if a boy they liked so much as said hello to her, she was suddenly "the problem." No matter what she wore or how she acted, she was "too much" of one thing or "not enough" of another. She was "the whore." She couldn't win with them. No matter how she dressed. No matter how she acted. She was always "too something" for someone. It was a constant moving target that left her exhausted, questioning herself, and always on edge.

The bullying continued despite complaints to the school, the parents, and the administration for years. Mental, emotional, social, and physical harassment and bullying persisted until she started to realize it was unhealthy.

They mocked her, her weight, her clothes, and her looks. They twisted her kindness into something fake. They'd gang up in group chats, say things meant to break her spirit, then pretend like it was just a joke.

The cruelty seeped into the small, everyday moments of her life. She'd spend too long in front of the mirror, tugging at her shirt, doubting if she should even go out. A buzz on her phone could send her stomach into knots, not knowing if it would be another round of teasing hidden as "jokes." Sometimes she would laugh along, trying to mask the sting, but later she would curl up in her room, carrying words that cut deeper than anyone else could see.

We went to the school, to the parents, to anyone who would listen, but the pattern never stopped. Teachers could shuffle desks, counselors could hold talks, but the damage was already etched into her. They mocked her looks, her clothes, even her kindness, twisting it to seem fake, when being kind was who she truly was. Bit by bit, it chipped away at her sense of safety in the world.

She didn't understand it. How could she?

She just wanted to be loved. To have real friends. To belong.

And no matter how many times they hurt her, she forgave them.

Not because she didn't feel the pain, but because she had a heart too full of light to hold onto hate.

It was a dizzying, toxic loop: **Friend → Bully → Friend again.**

The worst part was the *whiplash* of it all.

Friends. Enemies. Friends again.

It was dizzying for her. Infuriating for me.

And because she had such a big, soft, forgiving heart, she let them back in. Again and again. Not because she wasn't hurt, but because she believed in people. She believed they'd change.

The bullying wasn't just verbal. It was emotional. Relational.

They'd isolate her. Then reel her back in. Then push her out again.

They used Snapchat stories and group chats like weapons. Inside jokes that weren't really jokes. "Accidental" posts. Making sure she saw them all.

She was often left in the middle.

Loved by many.

Targeted by a few.

Crushed by the confusion of both.

There were days she didn't eat lunch, said she wasn't hungry, but I knew better. There were nights she stayed in her room, quiet, her sparkle dimmed just enough for me to notice. There were times she'd say she didn't want to go to school, but couldn't really say why.

I'd always ask her to talk to me. I'd lie down in her room with her and pray with her. I'd ask about certain friends, situations, and classes, but Aubreigh was buttoned up by the time eighth grade rolled around.

She carried that hurt quietly. She didn't want to be a burden. And when she did open up, it was often brushed off by adults who thought it was just "typical middle school girl drama."

But it wasn't. It was soul-crushing. Some of it was subtle. Some of it was cruel. All of it is damaging. And in the end, the reason why she left as early as she did.

By the time she started recognizing that this wasn't friendship, that it was toxic and unhealthy, she had already endured years of it. Years of mental and emotional warfare disguised as "just joking." Years of being worn down by the people who should have stood beside her.

For Aubreigh, middle school wasn't just about grades or dances or TikToks like it should have been. It was survival. Survival in the hallways, survival in her phone, survival in the very spaces that were supposed to feel safe.

And despite everything that happened from 5th to 7th grade, every whisper, every betrayal, every cruel message, Aubreigh was still optimistic about the new school year.

That was just who she was then. Hopeful. Resilient. She tried to lift others up, even though she herself was hurting. And her close friends knew her pain. They were there alongside her through the ridicule and the hatred. Despite the drama and being left out of a lot, we were still grateful that she had a few really close friends. Good solid ones. The kind that gave her belly laughs and inside jokes. And in Aubreigh's world, those few bright lights always seemed to outweigh the shadows. She clung to that hope. She chose to see the good. She *wanted* to see the good.

We lived in a small town. There was only one middle school option for our town. Changing schools wasn't just complicated; it was nearly impossible. As a single parent, and a teacher, I couldn't be in four different places at the same time. I looked into where else she could go to school, but didn't have anyone to take her.

And to make it more complex, I worked for the school district. I had to tread lightly, carefully trying to protect her while still keeping the job that paid our bills and put food on the table. I had other children to raise.

We talked about switching schools. It wasn't off the table. But the logistics were a mess. How would she get there? Who would take her? I worked full-time. I couldn't be in two places at once. As a single mom trying to make the best decision for *all* of my kids, it felt like an impossible equation.

And Aubreigh... she wasn't sure either.

Some days, she was adamant she didn't want to leave. She *wanted* to stay. She didn't want to start over. She didn't want to leave her real friends, who had stood by her, made her laugh, and made her feel seen. Other days, she wavered. She'd say maybe she did want to go. Maybe it would be better.

She went back and forth, and I know now it wasn't indecisiveness. It was *her* trying to figure it out, just like I was. She was trying to weigh where the pain ended and where the healing might begin. She was trying to be brave even when her world felt unpredictable.

And between you and me, I'll always question that decision.

If I had moved her, would it have made a difference?

Maybe I should've taken the choice out of her hands. Perhaps I shouldn't have let her decide. But it never felt that simple. It wasn't just a matter of enrolling her somewhere else. Housing, transportation, job stability, and the lives of three kids were at stake.

People on the outside like to say what they would've done. But they didn't live in our house. They didn't feel the weight of my every breath, wondering how to fix something that felt unfixable. They didn't see the way she lit up with her true friends, the way she still laughed at silly memes, the way she still decorated her folders with stickers and doodled in the margins of her notebooks.

They didn't see that she was still trying. Still believing.

They didn't see the hope.

And that's what makes this so complicated. It wasn't all darkness. There was still light. There was still love. There was still laughter. And that made it even harder to know what to do because for every ounce of pain she carried, she still clung to joy.

So, no, it wasn't simple. It wasn't obvious. It wasn't black and white.

It was messy. Complicated. Human.

And I carry that with me. Every day.

Despite that, we had hope for a great year! Through most of the day, everything seemed fine.

We texted back and forth just like any mom and daughter would.

At 10:35 a.m., I sent:

> How's your day going?

She replied:

> It's ok.

At 12:08 p.m., she texted again:

> I'm so ready for the day to be over.

I asked her why.

> Bc it's boring.

Typical. Middle school boredom. There was nothing in those early messages that hinted at what was coming. Just the usual check-ins. Mom stuff. Me, hovering just enough.

But then everything changed at 2:40 p.m.

She sent a message I will never forget.

> Momma. I'm in class with him.

> I'm sitting in the bathroom. I'm about to have a panic attack.

My chest tightened. I couldn't breathe.

Not him.

Then she called me. I'm in the middle of my own class, but I know I have to answer this!

The boy who had sexually assaulted her.

The same boy we had reported. The same boy she had bravely spoken up about just months prior, and had been dismissed about.

The same boy who resulted in social media posts from people she trusted and liked that read, "Team Him" vs "Team Aubreigh."

So there he was, the boy...

The same boy the school had promised would be kept away from her.

There he was. Sitting in class with her. Like nothing had ever happened. Like her pain didn't matter.

Like her trauma was invisible.

She ran from class and locked herself in a bathroom stall. She was texting me while trying to steady her breathing.

I could feel the panic through the screen.

I didn't wait. I didn't pause. I immediately called the school *furious*. Shaking. Yelling.

Screaming at whoever picked up the phone:

"You get to my daughter *right now*. She is having a panic attack. Alone. In a bathroom. After YOU put her in a class with her abuser!"

And at the same time, I was texting her:

> I'm calling the school now.

> On the phone with them now. I yelled!!

> I told them you're not leaving that bathroom until he is removed.

She *replied:*

> I can't.

> I'm sitting.

She was paralyzed. Stuck in that tiny bathroom, spinning in fear, while I tried to fight through a phone line.

Eventually, they got to her.

They escorted her to the counselor's office, where she stayed shaken, embarrassed, and emotionally wrecked for over an hour.

And after all that, the school's response? They changed *her* schedule.

Not his.

Hers.

She was the one relocated. She was the one made to feel like the disruption. Like *she* had done something wrong. Again.

It was just another dismissal. Another wound. Another moment where the people who were supposed to protect her... didn't.

And even through all of that, she came home, quiet.

Tired.

But still smiling.

Still showing up.

Still trying.

I could feel her struggle. And as a mother, I did all I could to lift her spirits.

I did everything I could to steady her. I reassured her again and again that she had nothing to be ashamed of and that none of this was her fault. I told her she was strong, that she was loved, and that the truth of who she was could not be changed by the way others treated her. I tried to fill her world with reminders of joy.

She went to every football game, sleepover, or little event she was invited to, even when I worried or wanted to keep her close. I hoped that being around her true friends would help her see how adored she really was, and how much she mattered outside of the school walls; she would realize that the people inside the school walls who made her feel bad about herself were actually very small.

At home, I brought her little treasures like her favorite snacks, tiny trinkets that made her smile, and small things that told her: I see you. I'm thinking of you. You're worth celebrating, even on the ordinary days. Sometimes it was just a note, or a silly conversation to make her laugh when the heaviness tried to creep back in. Sometimes it simply gave her the space to curl up in her room and breathe, with me checking in just enough to remind her she wasn't alone.

They were little things, but they were what I had. Reassurance, permission to still be a kid, small gestures that whispered: It will be okay. You're going to be OK.

True to who she was, Aubreigh didn't let the shadow of that first day define her. She kept doing what she did best, finding light in the little moments, being silly, laughing with friends, and living as fully as she could in the space she had.

In the days after that traumatic first day after the bathroom panic attack, the call, the fight with the school, the scheduling change. Aubreigh eased back into her rhythm. Or at least, she tried to.

Despite everything, she didn't let the first day ruin her year. She kept her head up and kept going.

Aubreigh had been doing what she did best, living in the little moments, being silly, and making people laugh. Her texts during that time said it all: the random "bruhs," the "mommyy" when she wanted something, the plans for late-night hangouts, and movie nights where no one ever really watched the movie. She was still just a girl, 13 and hopeful, still finding joy in the comfort of family and friends. One night she texted, "we just finished uno" followed by "bruh i wonnnn ." Just that pure, unfiltered joy.

We had fallen into a rhythm. One that felt soft and sweet, even in its chaos. The kind of rhythm that makes you believe, even if just for a moment, that everything might be okay.

She was spending her days at school, and weekends bouncing between close friends, sleepovers filled with TikToks, and nights at home with us. When she was out, she'd text me random things that made no sense without context, inside jokes, TikTok lingo, just simple "bruh" messages.

She told me she was okay. She smiled with her whole face. She teased me about being a "mom mom." She wore my perfume, my attitude. She was a mirror reflecting my heart right back to me.

The days were full of tiny texts, big feelings, and a kind of normalcy that felt like a rope, keeping me tethered to peace. Aubreigh danced, laughed, made videos, and smiled for selfies.

I worried, as mothers always do, but she seemed fine and happy. But I also wanted to give her space, to breathe, to feel like a normal girl.

So, I let her go to sleepovers with girls we both trusted. I picked her up whenever she called. I made her favorite dinners. I watched her laugh with her siblings. I watched her be Aubreigh, glorious, beautiful, and trying so hard to be okay in a world that had not been kind to her.

I'd get:

> Mommyyy 😩 can you bring me water?
>
> Can I sleep w y'all?
>
> What we doing tmrw?

Little things. The things that make a house feel alive.

August seemed to be flying by, and we were quickly falling into the school schedules and daily routine.

- Wake up around 5:30 a.m.
- Get coffee.
- Do our hair and makeup.
- Get dressed.
- Pack lunches, if we did not do it the night before.
- All of the kids left early with me, around 6:45 a.m.
- I would drop Taylor off at her friend's house for her to ride with to the high school since the high school started later than the other schools.
- Aubreigh and Ryker would come with me to work. Aubreigh would catch the transfer bus. This was a bus for teachers' kids to get to the other schools. It was a nice convenience to have. This enabled me to be in my class by 7:00 a.m. for student arrival at 7:05 a.m.
- Ryker stayed in my classroom with me and finished his breakfast before going to his classroom.
- After school, Ryker and I would go pick Aubreigh up at 3:30 p.m.

After school, she'd do homework, play on her phone, and talk to friends. Ryker would run around outside with neighborhood kids, and I'd start dinner in the kitchen. Taylor usually got home later, full of her own high school stories. The girls had different friend groups, so they rarely overlapped socially. But at home, it was the usual teenage tug-of-war: borrowing clothes, bickering, laughing, slamming doors, asking for rides.

Every night, we had dinner together at the table. Always. We had our seats, even though they weren't assigned, we always sat in the same spots. We said the blessings, and then our little ritual that I had started when the girls were young: everyone had to share the best and worst parts of their day. That was our moment to connect. Our way of checking in and hearing about each other's day.

Some days, Aubreigh would say her day was "fine." Others, she'd sigh and say something like, "I don't think they like me anymore," about her friend group. It felt like normal teenage stuff. On-again, off-again friendships. Middle school heartbreaks. We talked about it a lot. I tried to give her guidance but also space. Taylor and Aubreigh would often talk about what they had planned for the upcoming weekend, adventures of the school day, school gossip, and sometimes even teacher gossip, while Ryker talked about his playground adventures. My parenting style was somewhere between nurturing and structured. Hands-on, but with enough distance to let them learn on their own, too.

Aubreigh told me everything about her thoughts, her feelings, and her friends' drama.

There were good days, too. Days when she came home laughing, excited about a school event or weekend plans. Days when she'd toss herself on my bed just to tell me something funny. We'd sing in the car. Make TikToks. Laugh at inside jokes like "Slay queen," or "Whooo!? Who asked?" She was quirky and playful. Full of life.

The Weekend Before

Friday afternoon, Aubreigh had wanted all of us to go to the local football game. She loved when we did things together, and this was no different. "Come on," she nudged. "It'll be fun if we all go!" But the sky had other plans. Thick clouds rolled in, thunder low in the distance, and the forecast looked grim. I didn't want to drag Ryker out in a storm, so I told her she could still go, even though we'd stay behind. She hesitated at first, but eventually got dressed and went, texting from the car about who was going and what everyone was wearing.

Not long after, the skies opened up and the rain came down in sheets. The kind of Southern summer storm that makes the air smell like wet asphalt and turns parking lots into puddles. She called me before the game even ended, asking to come home. She was soaked, but she was smiling when I picked her up.

"It's fine," she laughed, climbing into the car. "At least I got to go."

That night, she had hoped to stay the night with a friend, but it fell through. So we stayed home. And honestly, that was okay too. She slipped into pajamas, curled up on the couch, and we did what we did best, just existed together. No big plans, no pressure. Just home.

Saturday rolled around, and she had another sleepover planned this time with a different friend. I said yes, of course. She packed her bag, makeup, charger, and all the things. Overpacked per usual. As I dropped her off that afternoon, the moment took a comedic turn. I accidentally backed my car into their metal basketball pole. My heart dropped. I texted her in a flurry of panic: "Aubs! I hit the pole in their yard! Please tell them I'm so sorry!"

She was calm. She always was in moments like that. "It's fine, Mommy," she said, "Don't worry."

That night, she stayed up late with her friend, making TikToks, taking pictures, laughing loud enough to echo down hallways. They had snacks, silly inside jokes, and that teenager buzz that fills the air when girls are up way past bedtime, saying things they wouldn't in daylight.

Then Sunday came.

I had assignments due, my master's program was in full swing, and I needed to carve out a few hours of quiet. So when she texted asking if her friend could stay the night, I told her no. Monday was coming fast, and she had her first golf lessons scheduled. Golf was new for her. And Aubreigh was like that, always willing to try new things. Her heart belonged to cheer and gymnastics. That was her passion, but over the years, she had tried just about everything. Soccer, basketball, volleyball, tennis, horse riding, and even track. But now? Golf. She was curious about the world and brave enough to explore it, even when it pushed her outside of her comfort zone.

I worried her friend would be bored waiting through her golf lesson, so I said no to the sleepover. She was a little bummed. She had wanted her friend to stay over so badly. She had planned it in her mind another night of staying up late, whispering about boys, making TikToks, and laughing until her stomach hurt. But I had told her no. She was disappointed. I chalked it up to the usual teen frustration. Thirteen-year-olds never like to be told no, and Aubreigh was no different. She had big feelings and wasn't afraid to show them, especially when it came to her friends. But it didn't last long. She moved on.

Since I was working on schoolwork, I asked Nick, who was a longtime friend at the time, to pick her up for me. He was close with the kids, dependable, and always showed up when it mattered. He grabbed her from the sleepover, and we all ended up at his house for dinner that night.

By then, Nick had been a steady, familiar presence in our lives. He was the kind of friend who showed up without being asked. The kind who'd help fix something around the house, bring over dinner when he knew I was overwhelmed, or sit and talk with the kids like they were his own. He was just a family friend, someone who cared deeply for us.

We had talked about the possibility of more, but at the time, I wasn't ready. So we kept it simple. Honest. A friendship that meant a lot, even without a title. There was no weirdness, no pressure, just mutual respect, laughter, and support. He was good to the kids, and they adored him.

Nick's place quickly became a favorite for the kids. There was always good food, friends, and fun over there. Aubreigh especially loved it out there. "Are we going to Nick's?" she'd ask, already texting a friend to see if they could come along.

She loved the freedom, riding four-wheelers through the fields, fishing off the edge of the pond, getting dirty, and laughing hard. It was simple joy. No filters. Just fresh air and freedom, and in a world that had felt so heavy for her, those moments mattered. They were pockets of light.

It was easy. Familiar. Comfortable.

So, I met them up there for dinner. I completed my weekly assignments, and before the midnight due date! Lucky me!

Aubreigh was in a good mood, her face relaxed and happy. She talked about wanting a new makeup vanity and rearranging her room. She wanted it for Christmas. I, of course, was telling her to go ahead and add to the cart. I wanted to see! She had a vision, always.

As we were wrapping up the evening, before heading home, she mentioned a boy, a ninth grader, whom she wanted to go to prom with. Just casual as friends, and knowing Aubreigh, she wanted to go more for getting dressed up and the experience of prom.

"I'm going," she grinned, her eyes lighting up with that same confident spark she always had when she was determined about something. "It'll be fun, Mom. He's really sweet."

I laughed, already shaking my head. "Absolutely not. You are in eighth grade."

Her smile fell just a little. "But it's just a dance," she said, pushing gently, the way she did when she really wanted something. "Come on. I'm mature. You always say I'm mature."

"I don't care if you're mature," I replied, standing firm. "He's still a high schooler. And you're still my daughter. It's a no."

She groaned. She pouted. She did the whole teenage performance, dramatic sighs, flopping on the couch, even dragging poor Poppi (Nick's dad) into the mix.

"Poppi," she pleaded, "Would you let your daughter go to prom with a ninth grader if she were in eighth?"

He laughed nervously, clearly wanting no part of that battlefield, but she didn't let up. Aubreigh was persistent. She didn't throw tantrums; she negotiated. Relentlessly.

But I was headstrong. I wasn't budging. The answer was no.

She was definitely bummed about it, her mood shifting into that low-key sulk that every mom of a teenage girl knows too well. When we got home that evening, she disappeared into her room for a while. I gave her space, not worried. This wasn't anything out of the ordinary. Just a girl disappointed over a "no" she couldn't talk her way out of.

We got back home with dinner out of the way, everyone full and content. The kind of Sunday evening where nothing felt rushed. No one had homework last-minute or a meltdown over missing shoes. It was calm.

By around 9 p.m., things were winding down. My eyes were heavy. I could feel myself dozing off to sleep. The house had that soft stillness to it, the kind that comes after a full weekend and right before the new week begins. Aubreigh was still up, in her room, scrolling on her phone, TV on, bouncing between TikToks and texts from her friends.

Ryker and I curled up on the couch in the living room, the one with its back to the two front windows, facing the main wall where the TV was mounted. That wall also backed up to Aubreigh's bedroom. The second couch was pushed along the side of the living room, facing inward toward the kitchen but still within view of the TV. It was a cozy setup, a little mismatched, but it was ours. Our little 1,300 square foot home. It wasn't much, but we had made it ours.

Aubreigh was in her room, which was just beside the living room. Her door opened into the hallway, just off that main living room wall. That long hallway was the opening for hers, Ryker's, and Taylor's bedroom, and then circled back into the kitchen. A full circle.

From the couch, I could hear her TV now and then or the different sounds from the videos she was watching on her phone. Her door wasn't fully closed, so I'd occasionally hear her laugh, soft and bright, like a little bell ringing through the house.

The hallway from the kitchen curved slightly and fed into the dining room. Which then led to my room.

A little bit after 9 p.m., I nudged Ryker, who had fallen asleep on my arm, and stood up slowly. As we moved toward the hallway opening just to the left of the TV wall, I glanced toward Aubreigh's room.

I got Ryker up, yelled "love you" to Aubreigh through the walls. She yelled "love you" back. I turned off the lights and we went to bed.

A normal night in our house.

So full of love. So normal.

And I'd give anything to press rewind.

3

*I*T WAS LABOR DAY, 2023.

I was doing an online high-intensity internal workout, something I had just gotten into. A little piece of structure, of trying to be healthy. I pulled my long blonde hair back in a ponytail and adjusted my black sports bra.

Ryker had wandered off to my room with his iPad. Looking back, thank God. He didn't want to be near the music of my workout because he couldn't hear his video. Little miracles. Little ways God was already working

I was maybe five minutes in, just finishing the warm-up. I was hot, and that stuck out to me because normally, Aubreigh would already have turned the air down before bed. She hated being warm. She always thought it was hot. I didn't like being cold. So she would often get up and turn the air down after I went to bed. It's just something she always did. But the house was still warm, which felt... strange. Not alarming, just different.

I walked to adjust the thermostat. The thermostat was in the hallway that branched off from the living room. And then

Out of the corner of my eye, I saw her vanity on the floor.

I laughed to myself, just a little.

Oh my goodness, girl, I thought. *You're already taking it apart.*

She'd just been adding new vanities to the Amazon cart the day before, showing me which ones she liked, dreaming out loud about which one might be her early Christmas present. Christmas was still months away, but that was just how we were. If she wanted something and I could make it happen, I did. She knew it. I knew it. That was our thing.

So when I saw the vanity on the ground, my first thought wasn't fear. It was her being her, a little ahead of herself, already assuming I was going to order the new one, as I often did.

It's funny now, in a way I can barely admit, that I thought that in those two seconds.

But everything changed in the next breath.

And then I saw her legs.

Purple.

Mottled.

Hanging.

Head tilted.

Not moving.

My first thought? *Leggings.* Just leggings. *It has to be purple leggings.* My brain just... couldn't process it. I now **hate** the color purple.

What I know now, but couldn't grasp then, is that when someone passes from hanging, the pressure cuts off blood circulation. Gravity causes the blood to settle in the lower parts of the body, and without the heart pumping, the blood pools. It turns the skin purple, marbled, bruised-looking. It's called *livor mortis,* one of the early signs after death. This is often called lividity as well. The color will stay even when rigor mortis sets in.

But at that moment, I didn't think about it medically. I didn't think logically. I thought like a mother.

Everything inside me shattered.

But in those first few seconds, the thought that she might be gone didn't even cross my mind.

This was an attempt, I told myself. *I can save her. I can get her down. I can fix this.*

There wasn't time to panic. I just moved.

I ran to her. I tried to lift her. I wrapped my arms around her legs and held her up, trying desperately to create slack in the rope. My hands were shaking. My voice broke open.

I screamed

"TAYLOR!!"

Taylor came running. Panic set in. I screamed at her to grab a knife, but it was too dull. I tried and tried to cut the rope while holding Aubreigh up.

WHO HAS A DULL KNIFE!!!

I was still holding Aubreigh, my arms around her body, my soul screaming. Taylor ran again fast and brought back another knife. She cut the rope, and Aubreigh collapsed onto me. Her whole body fell onto me.

I laid her on the bed. Her legs were dangling. Her feet were purple. I hate purple.

I tried to think. Circulation. I had to help with circulation. I grabbed the vanity stool and propped her legs up. I started CPR.

I had been trained. I remembered the instructions to *push hard.* Hard enough to break ribs if necessary. So I did. I pushed and pushed. Fluid came from her mouth, and I thought it was vomit at first, but it wasn't. I didn't stop.

Taylor was on the phone with 911. I could hear her and not hear her at the same time. Everything was happening all at once, and yet nothing was moving fast enough.

I kept going. I kept trying. And then the police pulled up. I collapsed beside her.

Her face was cold.

Her legs, her toes… a color I can't even put into words.

Her hands were rigid.

And still, I couldn't believe she wasn't coming back.

I screamed at them, **"GIVE HER OXYGEN!"**

I begged God. Begged.

"Please give her back. You've brought others back. Bring her back to me. Please God, bring her back."

I refused to leave her. Lying beside her, I cradled her face in my hand, kissed her cheek, and stayed with her.

Then my best friend Nick arrived.

Then my brother Jeff.

Time blurred. My body was there, but my soul was cracked wide open.

A police officer stayed in the room with me. He didn't say much; he just stood there, quietly letting me be with her. Maybe he knew there was no separating a mother from her child in that moment.

Time passed. I don't know how much.

Then the investigator arrived.

They needed to get in the room. They needed me to leave. Initially, I refused. I was going to lie there and die from heartbreak with her. I was never leaving.

They pleaded with me, Nick, Taylor, and Jeff. The officers assured me I would get to go back in there and be with her. I wasn't ready. I needed more time. More of her.

They nearly begged me. Almost had to drag me, though not physically. My soul had to be torn away.

I made them **promise** that I could come back to her.

And only then did I move.

I walked out of Aubreigh's room and back into the living room. I saw the weights from my workout, and I picked them up and threw them with everything I had.

Oh, the irony that they, too, were purple.

I **hate** purple.

The floor cracked. I collapsed.

I just fell to the floor, into myself. My knees pulled up to my chest, arms wrapped tight around them like I was trying to hold myself together because everything inside me was breaking apart.

My back curved forward, shoulders trembling, chin pressed down. I folded into the smallest shape I could make, as if I made myself small enough, I could hide from the pain, as if shrinking would make the world less heavy, as if curling inward could stitch the broken parts together.

My hands crawled up my face, fingers tangling in my hair, gripping my scalp as if I could physically wrench myself awake from the nightmare. I rocked the way a child does when they need to be soothed, an instinctive, useless motion. There was no comfort, only the raw, hot pain that burned behind my eyes, in my throat, in the hollow of my stomach. Every breath felt like a mile; each inhale a struggle, each exhale another piece of me gone.

But there's no comfort in a moment like that.

I was balled up on the floor. A mother shattered into pieces. No words. No oxygen. No time. Just prayer, and the kind of grief that lives in your bones.

That position wasn't just physical; it was spiritual.

I felt like I was lower than the ground. The heaviness weighed on me, making it hard to exhale. I was stripped of everything but the ache.

And I stayed there because there was nowhere else to be.

Sound came out of me, the kind of sound that doesn't come from your throat; it comes from the soul. A scream that clawed its way out of me, not a cry, not a sob, but a wail, screams from the depths of my soul, a mother's soul. One that never really stops, screams that seemed to lift from the deepest place inside my bones. It wasn't a sound I recognized; it was older and fiercer than language. I let it roar, taking sips of air when I could. I rocked back and forth. My body convulsed with sobs and sounds I couldn't control. My forehead pressed into and against the ground, like I was trying to bury myself in it. Trying to disappear and trying to sink into something that didn't feel like this nightmare.

I let the scream go until my voice rattled and I could only take small, jagged sips of air, the tremors running through my limbs.

No words. Just pain. Wailing from a place I didn't know existed inside me. People moved around me, voices, questions, shoes on tile, but it was all far away, like a radio turned to a station I couldn't reach. Everything blurred into the ache: There were police officers, EMTs, investigators, and strangers with so many questions. But I couldn't hear any of it clearly. Everything was blurry. My soul was screaming too loud for anything else to make sense.

The coroner arrived, someone I had gone to high school with, of all people. Names and faces, questions that I could not focus on. All that mattered was the hollow where my daughter used to be, the tiny space that used to hold her laugh. I stayed on the floor because there was nowhere else that felt like the right place to be; my body was doing the only thing it could to contain a grief that wanted to spill me out. No words could hold it.

Seconds, Minutes, time was passing. I wanted back in the room. I needed her!

The investigator was done, and the coroner went in to do their part. I stayed outside, restless. I didn't know what happened behind that door, and maybe I didn't want to. All I knew was that it was keeping me from her.

Finally.

They told me I could go back in. I didn't know exactly what had taken place in that room while I waited, and maybe I didn't need to.

The chaos from before, where everything had been toppled, was gone. I took in the room in a few slow, terrible seconds: the vanity upright, the scattered things gone. Someone had straightened things up. In its place was a heartbreaking kind of stillness. My eyes found her instantly. She had been gently turned, her head placed onto her pillow, her blanket pulled up and tucked around her small frame. Her head rested as though someone had just come in to say goodnight. For a moment, she looked, impossibly, like she was sleeping. It almost looked like I could lean down, whisper her name, and she might stir.

I sat on her vanity stool right beside her bed because I did not know where else to sit. I stared until my eyes burned, and then I reached. I touched her skin like I was trying to check whether she was real. I held her hands as if I could press breath back into them. I brushed hair from her face and kissed the soft places on her cheek until each kiss felt like a small, private promise. I just stared at her. I memorized the slope of her nose, the line of her jaw, the way her lashes lay like little shadows. I knew it would be the last time I'd ever see her in our home. In her home. In the home where I loved her and raised her. In that place, I thought she felt safe because she was in that home. I kept saying every small thing to myself so that later, when the room emptied and the world tried to move on, I would still have each detail.

Time didn't move in minutes anymore; it bent and blurred. I don't know how long I sat there, only that at some point the coroner came in and spoke to me in a voice both gentle and impossibly practical. When I was ready, he said they would be taking her to the funeral home. I saw a stretcher at the edge of my vision, the clinical wheel of it moving like a clock I could not stop. The room, which a moment before had held every ordinary piece of our life, began to shrink around that single fact: I would have to make decisions next.

Decisions. About my daughter. My baby. A human I had grown and raised and loved with everything in me. Now she was a body that needed arrangements. Nothing made sense. My soul couldn't comprehend it. My body couldn't process it. My mind refused to.

I let go of Aubreigh's body, walked into the living room, and allowed them the space to put her in the body bag. And she was quickly moved onto a stretcher. As they rolled her out into the living room, they paused and started to zip it up. I rushed back over to her. I lay over her, refusing to let them zip her face into a bag. My brother Jeff and Nick gently pulled me off of Aubreigh, and I stood next to them, frozen as I watched the authorities take my baby girl away.

I just watched. I watched my baby leave our home. I watched her leave, knowing she would never come back through that door again.

I just stared. Frozen. Blank. Hollow.

I don't remember much more of that day. It blurs and fades.

People's faces were around me, polite, practiced, asking questions I could not answer: "Who should we call?", "What can we do?" I heard the words, like someone speaking through water, but my head was full of nothing. They asked me practical things because that is what adults do in moments they cannot live inside: "What are you going to tell Ryker?" I hadn't even reached that corner of my mind. My despair had swallowed everything. I couldn't see past the breadth of my own pain to imagine how to shape words for a six-year-old. I hadn't even thought that far. My despair had swallowed everything.

So while the rest of the house was heavy with devastation, in that back bedroom, there was this strange stillness, almost sacred. Ryker stayed safe and undisturbed, wrapped in more than just his blanket—wrapped in love, in watchfulness, and in a peace that could only have been divine.

Somehow, Ryker didn't hear a thing.

He was in my bedroom, the farthest room from the living room and from Aubreigh's room. Taylor was there, moving in and out like a quiet guard, checking on him over and over. She was just a girl herself, but that day she was in full action, slipping in every now and then to ask, *"Are you hungry? Are you thirsty? Do you need anything?"*

But Ryker—no questions. No wandering. No interruptions. No awareness.

That was unheard of for Ryker. Normally, he'd be by my side in an instant, needing me, asking what was going on, being a busybody. But not that day.

And I *know* God was with him. I believe with everything in me that God, or Jesus, lay beside Ryker in that bed. He wrapped him in peace, comfort, and protection so strongly that nothing could reach him, not even the screams of his mother.

Not the chaos. Not the devastation happening just a few walls away.

Maybe it was still Aubreigh's spirit in the house. Lying with him. Protecting him one last time.

Regardless, somehow and only by grace from above, Ryker stayed in that room, in that bed, for six hours.

It was a miracle.

A real, divine miracle.

When Taylor and I finally walked into his room around four, everything felt impossible to say. I sat on the edge of my bed and looked at my sweet six-year-old boy, Aubreigh's best friend, his hair mussed, his eyes wide with the oddness of the day. My voice broke before I could shape the sentence. "I have to tell you something," I said. It felt like the only sentence I could find.

He looked up, confused. Innocent.

"Sissy's not with us anymore," I said. "Aubreigh went to Heaven to be with Jesus."

He just stared at me. Confused. Quiet. And then he cried. It was more from the shock, from seeing us in pain, from the energy in the room. I don't think he fully understood just yet what I was talking about because later he would still walk through the house and look for her, expecting her to be in places she had always been: at the table, by the sink, in the doorway. That searching for that ordinary, hopeful habit of a child hit me like a fresh wound every time. He was still her best friend. He was still the little boy who wanted to play and be held and be told everything would be all right.

I don't remember the rest of that day in clear order. It all becomes a haze of slow movements and clipped conversations, of people arranging things that no longer mattered, and the hollow ritual of it all. It hadn't sunk in. How could it?

The worst thing that could happen to a family was happening to us. We never discussed something this complex and unimaginable before. It wouldn't. Not yet. Not for any of us.

The permanence... that part would take time, if ever.

That night, I lay in bed, eyes wide open, mind spinning, body trembling.

And I only had two thoughts. Two desperate, pleading prayers:

God, please take her to Heaven. God, please let it have been quick.

I just kept repeating those two things like a mantra to the Heavens.

I had always been taught that suicide meant Hell. If you take your own life, you can't ask for forgiveness; therefore, you don't go to Heaven.

And I begged God not to let that be true.

Please, Lord. She was a child. She loved You. She had such a kind heart. Please take her to Heaven. I will take her place if I have to. Please take her, God.

And then there was the second fear.

I had heard horror stories about how long it can take. The suffering. The gasping. The regret.

And I couldn't bear it. I couldn't live if I thought my baby struggled like that. I couldn't stop imagining the worst, as if it could get much worse. I couldn't survive if she had suffered in those last moments.

So I prayed again.

God, let it have been quick. Please. Please, God. Let it have been quick.

I even searched the internet for information about it. Searching for answers in the dark.

No rest. No peace.

Just pleading.

4

THE NEXT DAY, WE WENT TO THE FUNERAL HOME. THE ONE where they had first taken her.

I didn't understand how funeral homes worked. It was all new. All foreign. All unbearable.

On the drive there, still not even sure what a funeral home really did, my phone rang. It was a man I didn't know then, but who would later become a dear friend: Jeff O'Keefe.

Jeff worked for O'Keefe Funeral Home, based in Ocean Springs, our town, our home.

He had heard what happened and reached out.

We talked. He spoke to me with such calm, such warmth, such clarity.

He explained how things work, gently walking me through the process.

He didn't rush. He didn't push. He just supported.

And more than anything, he gave me peace.

What struck me most was that Aubreigh wasn't even at his funeral home. Jeff wasn't calling because he had to, or because it was part of his job. He reached out as a good person, as a fellow parent, as someone with mutual friends who simply wanted to help in the only way he could, by offering guidance and compassion in a moment when I was drowning.

I remember hanging up and telling myself *this feels right.* It felt like where Aubreigh should be.

However, Aubreigh was still at a different funeral home. So I thought, *Let's just go in, talk, and see how things go.*

We sat in the small, quiet room of the funeral home. The woman was kind and calm. But I was barely holding myself upright. Everything in my body felt heavy and numb, but my mind was racing.

There was one question I hadn't said out loud yet. One that had haunted me. The one I had pleaded with God!

I finally asked it, through a cracked voice and a throat dry from crying:

"Did she suffer?"

The woman looked at me with such stillness. I could see the answer already forming in her eyes, but she gave me the space to ask it. To need it.

She spoke gently, like someone who understood how fragile I was in that moment.

The woman looked at me, gently, and said, "No. Her neck was broken. She passed instantly."

I couldn't breathe. I stood there staring at her. Frozen.

She went on.

"Because her neck was broken, and there were no petechiae around her mouth or face, it means she passed instantly. She wouldn't have felt pain. She wouldn't have been scared. She didn't suffer."

And as horrible and tragic and unthinkable as it all was, I cried out in relief.

Because that had been my prayer. One of only two things I begged God for through an entire night without sleep.

Please, God, let her be in Heaven.

Please, God, let it have been quick.

I lay there, eyes wide open, trembling under the weight of what I'd seen. I kept picturing her struggling, gasping, repeating my prayer.

Please, God, let her be in Heaven.

Please, God, let her be in Heaven.

Please, God, let her be in Heaven.

Please, God, let it have been quick.

Please, God, let it have been quick.

Please, God, let it have been quick.

But this woman standing before me was giving me my answer. Clear. Medical. Merciful. As horrible and awful and devastating as it was, I thanked God because that meant my baby didn't suffer.

Thank you, Lord, for answering my prayer. Thank you, Lord, for giving my baby peace in her final moments on Earth. Thank you, Lord, for taking her to Heaven. Thank you, Lord, for being with her.

She hadn't suffered. She hadn't been in pain. She hadn't been gasping. She passed quickly.

She did not suffer. Her neck had broken high enough on her spine to sever the connection between her body and her brain. That meant her consciousness would have ended almost instantly. And the absence of petechiae, those tiny red marks that often show up when someone is slowly suffocated, confirmed it. Her body hadn't struggled long enough to show any of those signs.

It was fast. It was quiet. It was merciful. My 13-year-old daughter died quickly.

Even with the answered prayers and the gentle care we'd received, something still didn't sit right with me. The place didn't feel like home. It didn't feel like where Aubreigh should be.

It's hard to explain, almost impossible to put into words, but deep in my soul, I just knew.

There was nothing wrong with the funeral home or the people there. They were kind, respectful, and professional.

But it was in a different town, about 30 minutes from us, and I wanted her in our hometown. Our community, where she grew up. Ocean Springs, Mississippi, was Aubreigh. And I couldn't ignore that feeling.

After meeting with the director there and thanking them for all they had done, I walked out, my heart still unsettled. As soon as I got into the car, I called Jeff O'Keefe back. I told him that even though there was nothing wrong with the funeral home she was at, my heart was telling me something different. I wanted her closer. I wanted her home.

I told him the situation. "She's already been taken to another funeral home... what do we do now?"

Without hesitation, he said, "Don't worry. We'll take care of it. We'll go get her."

Just like that. No pressure. No stress. No added burden.

He lifted the weight off my shoulders and carried it like it was nothing.

That's who he was. That's how he handled every step that followed.

O'Keefe Funeral Home picked her up on September 5th, 2023, and brought her home to *our* funeral home.

There was no drama. No conflict. Just a quiet shift.

A gentle return to where she belonged.

The rest of that day drifts in pieces for me, people coming and going, phone calls I can't fully recall, hours that blurred together. What I remember most is the stillness that followed once decisions had been made. A strange calm, though heavy, settled over the house.

September 5th, 2023

And then came the next morning. September 5th, 2023. Pastors visited me at our home, as did our close friends and family. We were surrounded by love and support.

Still, the questions pressed on my heart. And I asked one of the pastors because it wouldn't leave my mind. "Is it true? What was I taught? That she's not in Heaven?"

And he told me something that brought peace to my soul.

He said, "People believe that because they think you have to ask for forgiveness right before you die. But if someone dies suddenly, like in a wreck, they don't get that chance either. Yet if they knew the Lord, they're still saved."

He explained that salvation isn't about one last moment, it's about *relationship*. About knowing and loving Jesus. About the heart. And in that moment, I knew with every fiber of my being, Aubreigh was in Heaven. He welcomed Aubreigh.

The same two prayers I begged God for with everything in me... He answered both.

Even in the depths of despair, he was there. He held Ryker the morning I found his sister. He gave Taylor the strength beyond her years to find the courage to stay calm and the wisdom to protect her brother while I was unraveling. And He met me in the mess with mercy.

By 2:00 p.m. on September 5th, it was time for something I had both longed for and dreaded. Nick, Taylor, and I were going to see Aubreigh for the first time since she had been at the house. I didn't want anyone besides us to see her for the first time. Our little tight-knit family. I knew she would be embalmed, so I prepared myself for her to look different. It took 20 minutes to get across town to where she was; no matter how hard I tried to calm myself, nothing worked.

I couldn't take deep breaths. My skin felt like it was crawling off my bones. My heart was heavy, and my throat was tight. I couldn't sit still or think straight.

We walked into the funeral home. Nick was practically holding me up as we walked in together. My legs felt like they didn't belong to me, like every step was borrowed strength. We were guided into a small office to meet with Jeff O'Keefe. It felt unreal to be sitting down at a desk, like this was some ordinary appointment, when everything in me was shattered. I wasn't prepared for the decisions that had to be made.

One by one, he walked us through them with such patience: the casket, the flowers, the guest book, the memorial cards, even the lining inside the casket and the blanket that would cover her. All the pieces that determined how and where she would be laid to rest. All the decisions I had never thought about suddenly stared me in the face. Each choice felt impossible, yet necessary. Every question asked of me was a reminder that this was real.

Afterward, Jeff moved us into another room. It was filled wall to wall with caskets, shelves of urns, books laid out with options for guest registries, memorial keepsakes, and more. All of it in one compact space. Too much for my soul to take in. I broke. My knees gave out beneath me, onto the floor in the doorway. Nick did his best to comfort me. He knelt beside me, doing his best to hold me together, whispering whatever words he could manage, but there was no comforting me. The weight was too much. The air itself felt too heavy to breathe. I was inconsolable. It was so hard to function, to think.

Still, I knew I had to keep going. I had to make decisions for her. For my baby. And I wanted to be strong—strong enough to choose what was worthy of her, strong enough to honor her life with the care she deserved. Even if every choice tore a new hole in me, I would not turn away. I had to make decisions for her. I wanted to be strong for her.

So with everything I could muster, I just started talking, letting my thoughts, ideas of what she would want, spill out one after another. Jeff kept pace with me, steady and patient, as if he knew I needed to release everything crowding my mind.

I can't stand the idea of her being in the ground with bugs.

Can I be there when you put on her makeup and get her dressed?

Do you think she suffered?

How do you know?

Jeff met me with answers as fast as I threw them out there. He had a cement vault I could buy, and her little casket would go inside of that. And they'd put the top of the vault on top of her casket.

And even though I had already heard that my baby hadn't suffered, I needed to hear it again. I needed reassurance. Jeff said the same thing I heard a few hours earlier.

Her neck had broken high enough on her spine to sever the connection between her body and her brain. There was no sign of petechiae, those tiny red marks that often show up when someone is slowly suffocated. Her body hadn't struggled long enough to show any of those signs.

Once I heard those words again, I could move into decisions. I picked out a white vault with pink swirls of glitter, a pale pink casket, and white accessories that she would have loved. Her sheets and pillows were white, and her guest book was the prettiest one they had. It was the only one she would have wanted.

Taylor was with me every step of the way and helped me make each and every decision, picking out things Aubreigh would have loved. My heart ached thinking of what it cost her to stand there, making impossible choices for her little sister, when really, they should have been picking out movies for Friday night, or planning what snacks to buy for a sleepover. They should have been talking about homecoming outfits, or borrowing each other's makeup, or arguing over which shirt belonged to whom. Instead, Taylor was helping me choose caskets and guest books. I couldn't stop thinking about what she was feeling, carrying a weight no teenager should ever carry. But I was so grateful she was there, helping me make unheard of choices for her baby sister.

After the last decision for the moment, Jeff moved into the viewing room so I could be with Aubreigh. He reminded me that they had to wash her hair after embalming, hoping I would be prepared. But I wasn't.

Jeff opened the doors to the viewing room where they had her laid out on a stainless steel table, but it was as tasteful as they could manage since Aubreigh didn't have a casket just yet. She was lying on a white sheet that draped to the floor. And she was covered in a white sheet with just her face exposed.

From the second Jeff opened the door, I could see her lifeless, colorless little beautiful body, and I knew from where I was standing, feet away from her, that she didn't look like my baby.

"NO. That's not her!" I screamed as I ran to her and fell onto her, wrapping my arms around her the best I could. She was cold and stiff, but she was mine, and she deserved more than that.

I wailed and cried like someone was ripping out parts of my spirit still left inside. I knew she was gone, but it was the first time I saw her since she left our home the morning before.

It was an emotional tornado, and Nick tried his best to comfort me, but there's no comforting a mom who's standing over her baby. He rubbed my back for a minute but left me. Taylor just stood there, silent and shattered, her hands resting on her sister. Ryker had been dropped off only moments before by his dad. He reached for Aubreigh's arm, small fingers clutching what he could, wanting time with his sissy. My grief spilled out as more questions, ragged and desperate.

Jeff O'Keefe did his best to meet each one with gentleness and explanation as I screamed out questions.

Why was her hair wet?

Why does she have cuts under her collarbone?

Why does she have a gigantic cut on her neck?

Then there was the question Ryker didn't have words for. He touched her hand, pulled back, and looked at me with wide, confused eyes. She was cold. She was cold to the touch, and Ryker didn't understand why.

"She's with Jesus now, honey. She passed away, so blood is not warming up her heart anymore," I said softly. He accepted it in the simple, trusting way only a child can.

I was grateful he accepted the answer. I pulled him close to me and kissed the top of his head, while still holding onto Aubreigh.

Time didn't exist in that room. I don't know how much time passed, but once I was able to collect myself enough to see straight and stop hyperventilating from crying, I wanted to examine her. I couldn't do it with all the emergency personnel in my home the day before.

I wanted to memorize every inch of her.

Her freckles.

The tone of her skin.

Her eyelashes.

The color of her hair.

Her hot pink acrylic nails.

As I walked around her body, I lifted the sheet to touch her feet and gasped at the sight of her legs and feet. Still purple. After I returned to her head, I wrapped my arms around her face and stayed there. Cheek to cheek. Whispering to my little girl that I loved her.

After some time, I knew it was time to leave, as Jeff needed to close up the funeral home for the day. I picked up Ryker so he could kiss her forehead, and we all said goodbye to Aubreigh. Before we walked out, Jeff gave me the next steps. He would be sending a template for her obituary and asked for photos of her to play on a slideshow.

Having Jeff there, guiding me step by step, was incredibly helpful. I don't think we could have done what had to be done without his help. I never planned a funeral before my baby's. I had only ever attended one funeral in my life and wasn't prepared for the number of things I had to talk about or decide at the pace I had to.

The next several days went by in a blur.

- September 6th, 2023—I had to pick out floral arrangements. Since her birthday is St. Patrick's Day, Aubreigh was obsessed with four-leaf clovers. Jeff said he could do pink four-leaf clovers to match her casket.

- September 6th, 2023—Taylor and I met with the headstone company. All I knew was that I wanted it massive. Aubreigh deserved something huge. I looked through selections and was immediately drawn to the black marble option. Turns out, most of America was as well, and due to the number of deaths in 2020 and 2021, black marble was on back order.

    Initially, I selected a teardrop, but it never felt right. When I learned I could have a butterfly, I changed it. Aubreigh would have loved the butterfly.

- September 6th, 2023—Jeff sent me her obituary and slideshow to approve.

- September 6th, 2023—We had a moral support meeting with the pastor from Aubreigh's church.

- September 7th, 2023—Keepsakes for the funeral brochures were finalized.

  God's Garden
  Must Be Beautiful
  God looked around the garden and found an empty space.
  He looked down upon the earth, and saw your tired face.
  He put His arms around you and lifted you to rest.
  God's garden must be beautiful for He only takes the best.
  He knew that you were weary, and He knew you were in pain.
  He knew that you would never be well on earth again.
  He saw the roads were getting rough, and the hills were hard to climb.
  So He closed your weary eyelids, and whispered peace be thine.
  Tomorrow
  When tomorrow starts without me, please try to understand,
  That Jesus came and called my name and took me by the hand.
  And when I walked through Heaven's gates, I felt so much at home.
  When God looked down and smiled at me, from His golden throne.
  He said, "This is eternity and all I've promised you.
  Today your life on earth is past and here it starts anew."

- September 7th, 2023—Taylor insists I change the photo of Aubreigh in the keepsake, as her sister would be so mad if I used her yearbook photo. I sent one more email to Jeff, and one more change was made.

- September 7th, 2023—Nick calls to remind Jeff and his team that Taylor and I want to be there for her final hair and makeup and to get her ready for her service.

- September 7th, 2023—Pick out her funeral outfit with Taylor. We were told to bring several options, and since she had cuts on her collarbone, we were instructed to bring high-neck options. I knew I wanted her buried in her white dress. It was her favorite. She wore it to the Megan Moroney concert. I grabbed a sweater just in case it wasn't appropriate with her cuts, and another dress, but I was pretty headstrong on that white dress. We grabbed some jewelry that she always loved and her gold earrings.

That night, September 7th, everything changed. Again. Taylor, Nick, Kassi, and I were sitting in the living room late at night, discussing what to expect the next day at the funeral home. Taylor was in constant communication with her friends, like most teenage girls. And she counted and leaned on them more than normal during that time of her life. I was grateful for her friends and didn't mind them texting or calling her at all hours of the night. So, when she got a notification on her phone at 10:30 at night, I didn't think twice. I knew it was a dear friend of hers checking in. Or at least, that's what I assumed.

It turned out that the group of girls who bullied Aubreigh took to a social media platform to post a video of a doll hanging herself and falling off a chair. The doll's face was red, with a red line traced down the doll's torso into her pubic area. One of the girls had her fingers in the shape of a gun next to the doll's head, and one of the legs was missing. There was a pink blanket draped over the chair with a white and pink dreamcatcher hanging from the door. Taylor's friends recorded it and sent it to her. Within a matter of seconds after seeing it, I had it saved on my phone and forwarded it to the school district superintendent with the names of the girls involved. And it was at that point that I made a big decision that would change the trajectory of my life, of *our* lives, really.

I wasn't going to sit back and let those girls hurt my little girl any further, making a mockery of her death; they had bullied her in life. I would not allow them to continue bullying her in her death!

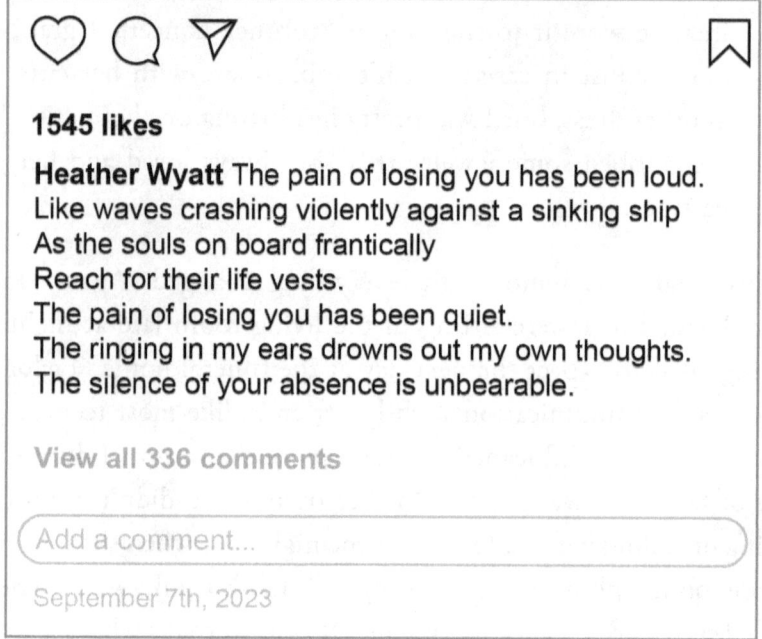

1545 likes

Heather Wyatt The pain of losing you has been loud.
Like waves crashing violently against a sinking ship
As the souls on board frantically
Reach for their life vests.
The pain of losing you has been quiet.
The ringing in my ears drowns out my own thoughts.
The silence of your absence is unbearable.

View all 336 comments

Add a comment...

September 7th, 2023

5

September 8th—Preparing Aubreigh

On Friday, September 8th, Taylor and I went to the funeral home. We had been given the privilege of getting Aubreigh ready for her funeral. Her last appearance. And as hard as that was for us, I was determined to be there for my baby every single second. She was, after all, only 13 years old, and the thought of her being exposed in front of strangers or someone else brushing her hair one last time made me come undone.

It felt both unbearable and sacred, one last chance to care for her, to mother her.

Aubreigh had left her Spotify logged in on my phone, a small treasure, so when we entered the quiet room where her body lay, I turned on her playlist. Her music filled the air. Her spirit was instantly there with us. And I could see her dancing to her favorite Megan Moroney songs. It was surreal. I didn't want that moment to be full of dread and something I'd look back on with nothing but sorrow in my heart. I don't know if that was my way of coping with the unimaginable or my undying love for my daughter.

The funeral home's makeup artist stayed close by, never doubting whether we could manage. She watched our every step. I didn't bother asking her if other clients brought in music or insisted on being with the deceased every step of the way. Her answer wouldn't have mattered or changed my mind. She was wonderful, patient, kind, and understanding.

She offered gentle guidance, explaining what could and couldn't be done. I respected her process and listened carefully as she described the limits to working with Aubreigh's skin when it came to makeup. Every day products wouldn't work. Things like foundation and mascara had to be replaced with a special kind that the funeral home provided. Still, she welcomed us to apply them ourselves using her products, letting us have that final act of care.

We wanted so badly to use the mascara Aubreigh always wore at home. She loved her eyelashes. They were her little piece of glamour. The makeup artist reminded us that only a particular type of black paint could be used on her lashes now. Regular mascara wasn't an option. I understood. We adjusted, determined to make her look as close to herself as possible.

Taylor and I then applied her lipstick. The same one she wore at home, the one that still carried the shape of her smile. My hand trembled as I steadied it against her chin, lining her lips with care. Her skin was so cold beneath my fingers, and I was careful not to smudge the makeup already in place.

As we worked, her music played softly from my phone, filling the quiet room. Between songs, tears fell, but there were also moments of laughter. Taylor and I told stories about Aubreigh—her sass, her humor, the sparkle she carried everywhere she went. We cried and we laughed, holding on to every little detail of who she was as we gave her this final gift of love.

Then came her hair. Curling Aubreigh's hair was one of the

greatest honors of my life, though it tore me in half at the same time. I stood over her, curling each section slowly, memorizing the way it felt between my fingers, the way the strands framed her face. I found myself studying her all over again. The curve of her eyelashes, the arch of her brows, the delicate shape of her ears. I traced the outline of her jaw, the way her hands rested so still. Little things I had seen a thousand times but wanted to etch into memory now, one last time. I studied her freckles, her lips, the gentle slope of her nose, the outline of her jaw. I was trying to burn every single detail into my memory, because I knew this was the last time. Every curl I finished felt like a prayer, a silent promise that I would carry her with me. It was unbearable, and yet it was sacred. The final act of mothering I could give her.

Finally, it was time to dress her. Taylor stepped out, and I understood. This was so much for her, and I didn't want her to carry more than she already had.

But for me, there was no question. This was my child. This was my task, my responsibility, my sacred duty as her mother. I was the one who brought her into this world, who clothed her for the first time, and I would be the one to clothe her for the last.

That day, I learned something: when you dress someone who has passed, you don't put clothes on them as you normally would. The back of the outfit is cut open, and you gently slide their arms through, tucking the fabric around them. I ensured we went very slowly, concentrating on every movement and being careful, respectful, and soft.

We dressed Aubreigh in her white dress, the same one she wore to the Megan Moroney concert just months before, laughing and dancing. Seeing her in it again was both unbearable and beautiful. Once she was ready, I called Taylor back in. Together, we listened to a few more songs, held her hand, and whispered our love. We knew it was the last time we would ever do this for her.

I lay my head next to hers and pressed my lips against her head.

My baby girl.

I couldn't believe she was gone.

Eventually, it was time to leave her. I knew I'd be back the next day, but leaving her wasn't easy. At that point, every step I took was painful, and every breath I drew in felt like betrayal. I was still living, and my girl was not. I couldn't protect her and keep her safe from the evil in this world.

And even though Aubreigh was lying dead at a funeral home, those girls who made her question her own worth still wouldn't leave her alone.

That night, Taylor learned that one of those girls had written something on Aubreigh's obituary page.

Taylor wasted no time at all.

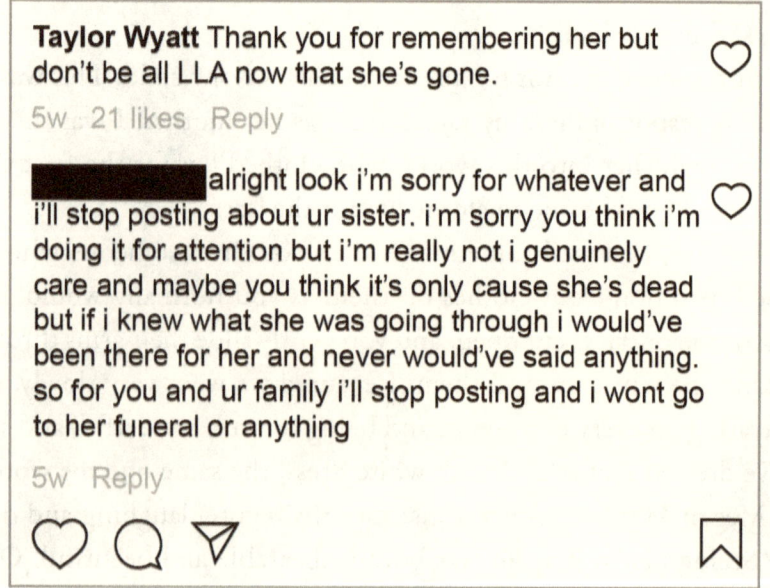

September 9th—One Last Visit

The next day, Saturday, September 9th, the funeral home gave us something they rarely offer: private time as a family. They explained that family moments always feel rushed on the day of a funeral. So they let us come in, just us, for a few hours. It wasn't the first time I saw the casket or her, but it was the first time I saw her in the casket.

It was me, Taylor, Ryker, my brother, her uncle, and Jeff. We stepped quietly into the room, while Nick waited outside to allow us our time, and we gathered around her, doing the things families do when words run out. We held her hands. We kissed her forehead. We stroked her arms. We sat together in the stillness, drawing close to her the way you would at a wake, only this time it was just for us. Ryker was restless in the way only a six-year-old can be, moving between sitting for a moment and then springing back up to touch her hand or lean down and kiss her cheek again. Over and over he returned, giving her gentle kisses. I couldn't stop him, and I didn't want to. It was his way of loving her, of saying goodbye. All I could do was hold him, hold her, and let the tears come. My little family together in one impossible moment.

The funeral home staff had learned how much Aubreigh loved Megan Moroney, and as we stood there, a speaker in the corner began to play *Tennessee Orange*. The first notes filled the room, and we all broke down. It was the sweetest gift, hearing her favorite song surround her one last time. For a few minutes, it felt like she was right there with us, smiling, singing along under her breath.

When it was finally time to leave, we walked out into the hallway and stopped in our tracks. The funeral home had brought in all the tributes that had been laid at the middle school: flowers upon flowers, posters covered in messages, stuffed animals, teddy bears, an outpouring of love transferred into one beautiful display. It was overwhelming in the best way. Every color, every note, every gesture whispered how deeply Aubreigh had been loved.

We stood there together, taking it in, breathing in the fragrance of plants and flowers, letting the sight soak into our hearts. It was beautiful. Painful, but beautiful. And then, with heavy steps, we turned to leave, carrying both the weight of our grief and the quiet comfort of having had that sacred time with her.

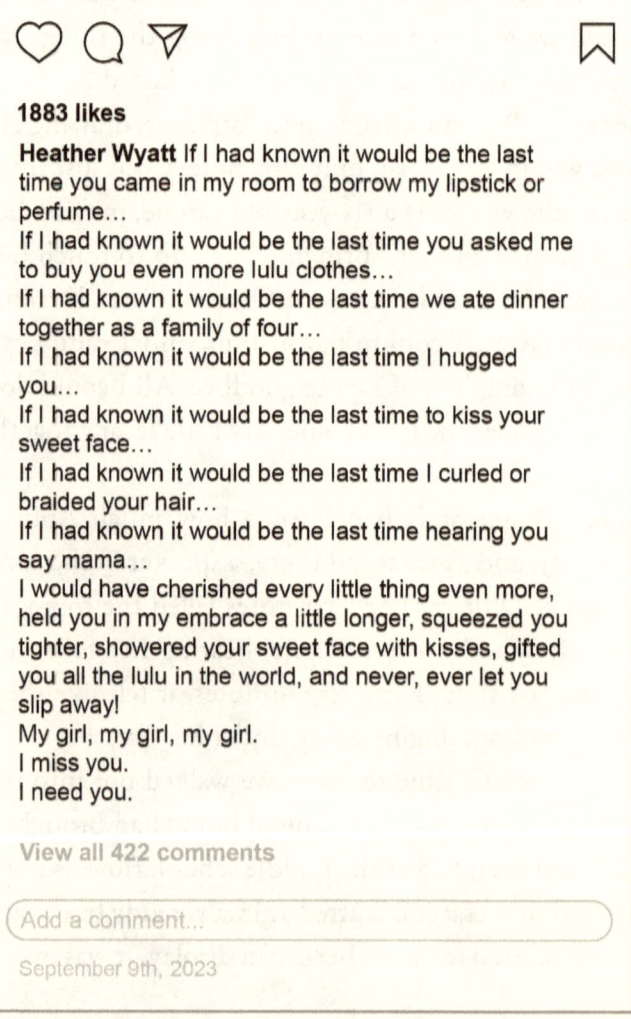

1883 likes

Heather Wyatt If I had known it would be the last time you came in my room to borrow my lipstick or perfume...
If I had known it would be the last time you asked me to buy you even more lulu clothes...
If I had known it would be the last time we ate dinner together as a family of four...
If I had known it would be the last time I hugged you...
If I had known it would be the last time to kiss your sweet face...
If I had known it would be the last time I curled or braided your hair...
If I had known it would be the last time hearing you say mama...
I would have cherished every little thing even more, held you in my embrace a little longer, squeezed you tighter, showered your sweet face with kisses, gifted you all the lulu in the world, and never, ever let you slip away!
My girl, my girl, my girl.
I miss you.
I need you.

View all 422 comments

Add a comment...

September 9th, 2023

60

September 10th—The Funeral

Sunday, September 10th, was her funeral. It felt like years had passed since she died, but really, it was only a week. In that time, so much happened, and every day seemed to stretch on endlessly. And every time I left the funeral home, I knew I'd be back another day to see her.

I didn't sleep much that week. Maybe a few minutes here and there, my body was trapped in chaos, fight-flight-freeze, alert, stress. Whenever I got into a sleep state, my nervous system ripped me back into reality. The night before her funeral was no different, except for the crushing awareness that the next day would be the last time I would physically see her.

I saw the sun crack through my bedroom blinds that morning. I rolled onto my side and clenched my chest and my belly and sobbed into my mattress. No sound. Just gut-wrenching convulsing.

When that passed, I went into autopilot mode. I splashed water on my face, made coffee, and got Ryker and Taylor up, but she was already moving around her room. The funeral wasn't until Noon, but I couldn't stand being in the house knowing Aubreigh was being moved, so we all got ready for the funeral.

Aubreigh's funeral was held right after the church's morning service, which meant we couldn't arrive until after the service was over and everyone had left. I knew how long it would take us to drive across town, and the kids were ready with plenty of time.

The drive across town was short, and the kids were ready well ahead of schedule. When we pulled into the church lot, I saw the funeral home vehicle parked quietly in the back. We parked beside it, then walked together to the side entrance of the church.

The entrance they guided us through led to a side room, not the main space, but a smaller one just off to the church hall. There were tables set up with water and refreshments, the kind of quiet hospitality churches are known for. On the wall, a PowerPoint slideshow of Aubreigh was already playing, picture after picture of her life glowing across the screen.

I walked in first and immediately broke down. I wanted to be strong for Aubreigh, but I needed a moment to feel everything. I wanted to be strong for her, but before I could step into the sanctuary itself, I needed that moment to feel everything. I knew her casket was waiting at the front of the sanctuary, but I hadn't seen it yet. For a few minutes, it was just this space, the side room, the looping images of her smile, the reminder of her life, holding me until I was steady enough to walk toward her.

After a few minutes, I was ready.

From the doorway, the view stretched long and narrow, pews lined neatly on either side, just like any church sanctuary, only this time, at the far end, my baby girl lay in her casket. I could see her even from the opening, framed by flowers and soft light. The space was perfect, almost too perfect. Pink touched every corner. Floral arrangements in the shape of four-leaf clovers, little details woven in that reflected who she was.

Taylor and Ryker were on either side of me as we stepped forward. None of us spoke; the only sound was our footsteps against the aisle. It was just me and my two surviving children, moving toward their sister. A mother, a daughter, and a son, walking together into the hardest goodbye of our lives.

I felt Taylor close in beside me, steady but trembling, holding herself together with every ounce of strength. On my other side, Ryker clutched my hand tight, small and restless, his eyes darting from the flowers to the casket, trying to make sense of something too big for him to understand. Soon after, we were joined by my brother, Nick, Kassi, and other family members. We gathered around, looking down at her, knowing these were our last earthly glimpses.

We spent about thirty minutes with her alone before I was told the off-duty police officers I had hired had arrived to stand as guards. Thankfully, the funeral home director met with them to discuss my instructions that cell phones and photography were prohibited inside her funeral. I emailed pictures of the handful of girls and parents who were forbidden from entering her funeral. Signs were posted on the church windows letting guests know they couldn't bring their phones or cameras in.

This wasn't to be documented or shared. And there was no way on God's green Earth I was going to allow those girls to make a mockery out of that day. Or my baby during the last time I'd see her beautiful face.

I glanced up at Jeff O'Keefe as he walked away from the security guards and gave a nod. I assumed that meant my wishes were going to be carried out, and I didn't have to worry that the girls who bullied my daughter were going to be sitting in front of me as I said goodbye to her.

People arrived shortly after the security guards took their spots at the church entrance. I saw them point to the signs in the windows a few times, and folks returning to their cars. I imagined the guards were instructing people to place their phones back in their cars.

When the service began, the three of us, me, Taylor, and Ryker, stood at the front beside her. Then came the people. One after another. Friend after friend. Family after family. The line stretched endlessly. Hundreds of people. Hug after hug after hug. My heart was grateful, but I was also numb, dissociating just to make it through. Ryker tried so hard to stay with us, but after a while, the weight was too much for his little body. He leaned against Taylor's side, his head heavy, his small frame worn out from the emotional toll. He was only six. He had been so strong, but he was exhausted, mentally, physically, emotionally. I knelt and whispered to him, "It's okay, buddy, you can sit for a while." He nodded, and we let him go rest on one of the front pews, where he could still see us.

That left just Taylor and me standing there, side by side, holding each other up as much as we held on to Aubreigh. Two broken pieces of the same heart, doing all we could to stay upright in front of her.

The line of visitors continued to come through: friends, family, teachers, neighbors, each one pausing at the casket, each one offering a hug or a kind word before moving on to their seat. Eventually, the sanctuary grew quiet again as everyone settled into the pews. It was nearly time for the service to begin.

That was when Jeff O'Keefe came to me. He asked gently if I wanted to step out for what came next, just for a moment, that it was time to close the casket.

I shook my head. "No. I'll be here for every single thing."

So I made my way to the front pew, with Taylor and Ryker on either side of me. As I sat down, my eyes never left her. I watched the funeral home staff, the men whose job it was to tend to these final details, step forward, their hands moving to prepare. And then, with the sanctuary hushed and everyone seated, they closed the top of her casket.

That heavy clank of the lid shutting into place. The finality of it split through me.

I ran to her and screamed, collapsing over the casket. The kind of scream that comes from the deepest part of your soul. Blood-curdling screams ripped from somewhere inside me that I didn't know existed. Several people, including Taylor, Nick, and my brother Jeff, all came up behind me, wrapping their arms around me, steadying me, trying to pull me from the casket. They guided me gently toward the side hall, holding me up as I broke apart, as I collapsed to the floor, balled up and crying.

Prayers rose up over me, voices mingling through my cries. Hands rested on my shoulders, my back, my arms. A cocoon of strength when mine was gone. I don't know how long I stayed there, only that the world felt suspended, sound and light blurring until at last I could breathe again, if only for a moment.

When I finally regained enough composure to stand, I walked back in. The service continued. One voice after another rose to honor her, words of love, stories of her light. I spoke. Taylor spoke. Taylor's dear friend Maddie, who had been like an additional sister, spoke. My brother spoke. Even her kindergarten teacher stood and shared. Each voice cracked and trembled, but each one carried her name with reverence. People sang. People wept. Together, it was both unbearable and beautiful.

And then, the time came. The pallbearers moved to the front, lifting her gently, carrying her down the aisle. We followed as they walked her out of the church and placed her in the waiting hearse.

The doors shut, and we began the procession. Vehicle after vehicle fell in line, headlights stretching behind us like a river of grief and love. I sat in the car and stared straight ahead at the one in front of me. The one carrying my baby. I could not look away for the entire forty-five-minute drive.

When we arrived at her resting place, the crowd gathered around quietly. The graveside service itself was brief; a few words, a prayer, and silence that felt heavier than any sermon. After the prayer, one by one, people drifted away. Doors closed, engines started, and cars pulled down the narrow cemetery road until the crowd was gone. For most, that was the natural end of the day. Their goodbye was said.

But not mine.

But I couldn't leave. Not yet. I stayed by her side, unwilling to turn my back on her resting place, even as the cemetery grew quieter and the crowd thinned to nothing.

And as they started to lower her into the ground, one by one, people left. Jeff asked if I wanted to leave, too.

The funeral staff came to me gently and asked if I was ready to leave, that I did not have to stay for the next part.

"No," I said. "I'm not leaving her."

So I stayed. With Taylor and Ryker by my side, close friends and family that had stayed off to the back to be there if we needed them, while the work began. I watched as the men stepped forward and turned the crank that lowered her casket slowly down into the vault already waiting in the earth. The chains creaked, the wheel turned, and I held my breath with every inch of descent. My eyes never left her. I wanted to see her through every last moment.

When her casket was finally settled into place, the men lifted a heavy cement vault cover and positioned it above her. They lowered it carefully until it rested over the casket, sealing it away. That sound, the thud of cement against stone, vibrated through my chest.

And then came the dirt. Shovel after shovel, scoops of earth hitting the vault. Each one echoed like it was striking my own body, my own heart. The sound was sharp, final, merciless. Still, I stood there, refusing to turn away. We watched until she was fully covered, until there was nothing left to see but earth.

I wanted to be there for every second, for every step, for every sound. It was my duty as her mother. To witness it. To stay. To not leave her alone.

And then it was over.

The last shovel of dirt was placed, the sound faded, and there was nothing left for me to do but stand there in disbelief. The cemetery grew quiet, and at some point, I knew we had to leave.

We walked back to the car in silence. My legs moved, but they felt heavy, like they didn't belong to me. Nick opened the door and drove us away, but my soul stayed behind, clinging to the ground where she now lay.

My body moved, but my soul didn't want to. Because now the

impossible had happened. I didn't just find my daughter hanging, already gone. I watched her be laid to rest in the Earth, where I couldn't go. I couldn't see her.

And I had to somehow go on with my life without her. I was expected to survive. Without her. Without my baby. Without the girl I made, raised, and loved with every breath.

I had to keep living. And right then, that day, I didn't want to. I wondered if I ever would. I knew I had to for Taylor and Ryker.

After September 10th, the days became a blur. Honestly, the weeks did, too. I was alive, I was breathing, but I wasn't really living; I was just existing. I had to send Ryker off to school like everything was normal, even though nothing would ever be normal again. Taylor stayed home longer, taking the time she desperately needed. But how could anyone just return to life as if it hadn't shattered?

At night, none of us could bear to be alone. I dragged a mattress into the living room, and every night we slept there together. We were too scared, too broken, too lonely to retreat to our separate rooms. Nightmares, scary, demonic faces haunted Taylor's nights; she couldn't escape. Ryker's tears soaked his pillow as reality finally began to sink in. Permanent. This wasn't a movie where someone comes back at the end. His sister wasn't coming back. How do you explain forever to a six-year-old? My brain couldn't even grasp forever.

So I lay there every night between my children, praying with them, holding them, begging God for strength. The days crawled forward, and eventually, Taylor went back to school. It was brutal; her anxiety spiked, and panic attacks followed her down every hallway. She felt like everyone's eyes were on her, whispering, staring. I stayed home. I couldn't yet return to work. I hid inside my house, whispering to myself: *This isn't my life. Please, God, let this not be my life.*

And when my mind went to a really dark place, it wasn't just grief I felt; it was the ache of remembering what had been done to her. My thoughts circled back to the bullying, to the cruelty she endured at the hands of girls who should have been her friends. I never called them by name publicly, and I still can't legally name them to this day. But the truth is, I don't have to. They know what they did. Their parents know what they did. And in a small town like ours, where nothing stays hidden for long, everyone knows. This wasn't just me "feeling rage." This was me staring into the reality of what had pushed my daughter into such a dark place. The relentless cruelty. The years of it. The way it followed her, seeped into her identity, convinced her she was unworthy of love, of life. It is impossible for me to think of losing her without also thinking of what she carried, what was done to her, and how those wounds shaped her final moments.

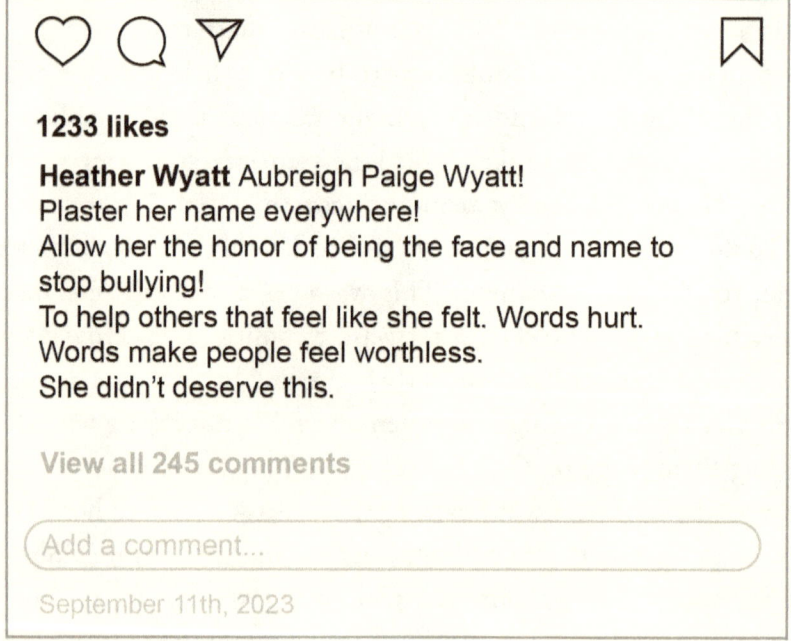

1233 likes

Heather Wyatt Aubreigh Paige Wyatt!
Plaster her name everywhere!
Allow her the honor of being the face and name to stop bullying!
To help others that feel like she felt. Words hurt.
Words make people feel worthless.
She didn't deserve this.

View all 245 comments

Add a comment...

September 11th, 2023

♡ ○ ◁   ⊻

1376 likes

Heather Wyatt My heart!!
The homecoming parade was amazing. They
dedicated a float to my girl! And my baby boy got to
ride in it! He loved it. I'm so grateful to everyone!

View all 266 comments

Add a comment...

September 14th, 2023

♡ ○ ◁   ⊻

2387 likes

Heather Wyatt My baby deserved more! She
deserved better!
A life gone too soon.
Raise awareness. Teach your kids.
Just be kind.
Talk to your kids.
Don't be passive.
YOU are your child's advocate. Do not tolerate any
form of bullying.

View all 413 comments

Add a comment...

September 14th, 2023

6

*I*N THE DAYS AFTER THE FUNERAL, LIFE MOVED IN STRANGE rhythms. I was deep in grief, barely functioning, yet at the same time thrust into constant conversations with the systems I had no choice but to trust—the school, the police, the district. Questions had to be answered. Reports had to be made. Meetings and calls came one after another. I clung to the hope that this time, finally, something would be done. That there would be accountability. That justice of some kind would come.

Meanwhile, I was still doing the everyday things that grief doesn't pause for: caring for Ryker and Taylor, eating when I could, rarely sleeping. It felt like I was simply maintaining, moving through the days with no real sense of time, just existing in the space between devastation and duty.

And in that space, connection came. Jeff O'Keefe introduced me to another mom who had lost her daughter to suicide. Her daughter had been in her twenties, but loss is loss. She and I became fast friends, bound by something we never wanted to share but understood without explanation. We didn't have to say much; we just knew.

She told me about a local walk being put on by the American Foundation of Suicide Prevention, and she invited me to join her. I wasn't sure that I was up for a public appearance or interested in being around others just yet, but I agreed to at least make an appearance.

There, she introduced me to others, families and individuals who knew this grief firsthand, who had walked through the same kind of loss. They didn't need me to explain, because they already understood. It was the strangest kind of comfort: being surrounded by people I had never met, yet who could look at me and see exactly where I was standing in my pain.

I met another family while there, a mother, a father, and their daughter, who had lost their son and brother not long before Aubreigh. They quickly became friends, people who knew this language of loss without needing me to translate it.

One piece of advice the father gave me still stays with me. He said something along the lines of, "Grief is like being stuck in the middle of the ocean, and then the waves come. Sometimes small, sometimes so powerful they crash over your head, one after another, shoving you under until you can barely breathe. Just when you think you've gotten your head above water, another breaks over you. There are days when the waves feel endless, when you're certain you can't keep fighting them. And then there will be days when the sea calms, just enough that you can float, catch your breath, and remember you're still alive. But the waves never disappear. They always come back."

It's a dark analogy, but it's true.

You never get out of the ocean. Some days the waves are bigger, harder, and faster, and some days they are more manageable. But either way, that's grief. You never get out of the ocean; you just learn to survive in it.

We didn't stay long at the walk, but I was thankful for it. Grateful, even. In that short time, we met people, exchanged stories, and gathered a handful of contacts, names, numbers, and cards I tucked away like lifelines. We kept in touch with a few of those families, and that ended up being one of the best gifts to this day.

Through those conversations, I was connected with a local psychiatric and therapy office, a community of professionals who understood grief and trauma. It felt like the very thing I had been searching for without knowing where to begin.

It didn't take us long to get appointments. I scheduled Taylor with one psychiatrist and me with another. Ryker was already scheduled with another therapist outside of that office to fit his needs better, with him being so young.

So another visit, more therapy. Hoping to start healing. It was September 18th, 2023. Taylor and I sat in double bench seats, bracing ourselves for yet another appointment with our psychiatrists, completing the standard questionnaires about our enjoyment of life, or lack thereof, lately, and self-harm levels, the weight of my grief still pressing against my chest like an anchor I couldn't lift. My thoughts were tangled, looping endlessly between the memories of Aubreigh's laughter and the unbearable silence she left behind.

That's when a mother approached me, behind her, seated a young girl, Aubreigh's age, with sad eyes, shy, and a look of defeat. The woman's voice trembled as she approached and apologized for doing so. She knew who I was and what happened to Aubreigh, and she told me her daughter was struggling. She asked for my advice, her eyes silently pleading for answers I didn't think I had. She explained that her daughter was going through bullying situations at school and was struggling with self-harm and suicidal thoughts.

I was still on guard because so many people, media members included, wanted to talk to me about Aubreigh, the girls who bullied her, and wanted to speak to me. I always refused. I wasn't ready to talk about it publicly just yet.

It wasn't uncommon for people to approach me in public, like at football games or grocery stores. And once, a member of the local newspaper misrepresented herself, and thankfully, a friend was nearby and stepped in before I said anything to her.

But in therapy that day, being asked for advice about a teen girl struggling with suicidal thoughts was new for me.

My first thought was sharp and cruel to myself: *What could I possibly tell her? I couldn't even save my child.* But before the shame could swallow me, something stirred deep within my spirit. It was as if the Lord Himself leaned in close, urging me to open my mouth, to let my brokenness speak.

So I did.

I told that sweet mama everything I wished I had done differently, every "would have," every "could have," every "should have" that I carried like stones in my chest. I poured out the lessons I had learned in the most painful way possible, hoping they might become her lifeline. My words would never bring my baby back, but maybe, just maybe, they could spare another family from standing where I stood. The spark was the quiet exchange between two mothers clinging to hope in the middle of a waiting room. It was the first moment I understood that my pain could be more than a wound. It could be a purpose. That's when the idea initially took root. Like the Lord himself spoke to me. I could do something. I could speak out. I could maybe make a change.

And later, after our appointments, on the drive home, something shifted. I replayed the conversation I'd had with that other mother, her brokenness echoing my own. For the first time, I saw a faint outline of purpose through the haze of grief. How could I reach more women like that mama? How could I take this ache and make something of it? I didn't realize it just then, but that quiet, trembling conversation planted the seed for something bigger than myself. In between my own appointments and Taylor's, in between the weight of grief and the cautiousness of sharing. That quiet, trembling exchange planted the first seed of what would become The Aubreigh Wyatt Foundation. If I couldn't save Aubreigh, maybe I could help save someone else's child.

A little while later that afternoon, a local attorney contacted me, asking if I wanted to meet him at his office and investigate potential lawsuits against the families and the school district.

I was posting on social media, pouring out pieces of my grief, heartbreak, and devastation. But it wasn't enough. I needed accountability, answers, and those responsible to face what they had done and what they had pushed Aubreigh into. I needed the truth. I needed action. I needed accountability for what my daughter had been pushed to do.

My immediate response to that individual was a big YES. We scheduled an appointment for the very next day.

He asked me to bring him everything I had: every document, every message, every screenshot. I handed it over to the police already. And I was glad to give him what I had, and it was easily attainable because I kept records of everything. I had the dates I had talked to the school, text messages from my and Aubreigh's phones, screenshots, videos, emails, the girls mocking her hanging, and I was glad to give it to the lawyer. I didn't care how much it was going to cost me. I'd find a way to pay for it to get justice for my girl.

I went to work making a long list of all the occurrences in which Aubreigh was bullied and asked for help. I went back to 2020.

2020

- *Sleepover with a few girls where inappropriate photos/videos were taken of Aubreigh while she was changing. She became emotionally distraught and feared the content would be shared. Parents notified.*

- *Aubreigh began enduring bullying, cyberbullying, and abuse by a group of girls through phones and in school.*

- *I advised Aubreigh to distance herself from one of the girls due to emotional stress.*

- *Continued tension among friends, with accusations of exclusion and misunderstandings.*

- *Sleepover at another girl's house. During the night, the girls sent inappropriate pictures to strangers on Omegle. Aubreigh refused to participate and was mocked and filmed while crying. She contacted me, and Aubreigh was picked up. Parents were notified.*

2021

- *At school, Aubreigh felt distressed, mocked. Screenshots later showed her resistance while the others taunted her. Notes were being passed around about her.*

- *One girl created and shared a threatening video targeting Aubreigh during school hours. Aubreigh reported it to her teacher and principal. That student was sent home for the day for harassment, but the bullying continued.*

- *I emailed teachers and the principal, reporting ongoing bullying:*

- ***Physical aggression:*** *Aubreigh being hit in the face.*

- ***Verbal abuse:*** *Name-calling and rumor spreading.*

- ***Online harassment:*** *Mocking TikToks calling her out.*

Teachers acknowledged the seriousness, apologized, and said the administration would act immediately (emails provided).

*Around this same time, **teachers themselves began reaching out**. They had seen enough to know how serious the situation was becoming. They admitted that the individuals targeting Aubreigh were engaging in "mean girl" behavior that was spreading through the grade. Some teachers quietly acknowledged their hands were tied, that they had escalated the concerns, but nothing meaningful was being done. They also noted that Aubreigh wasn't the only one. These same individuals were treating other students cruelly as well.*

- *Teachers expressed apologies and sympathy, promising to keep an eye on things and to continue reporting up the chain, but their frustration was clear: the system wasn't protecting Aubreigh.*

- *Aubreigh's body and weight were mocked by one of the girls. A substitute teacher was present, and no action was taken. (Email and evidence provided)*

- *Cyberbullying escalated on Snapchat and TikTok. Mocking videos of Aubreigh's voice, clothes, and appearance circulated. Despite repeated reports to the counselor and principal, no meaningful action was taken.*

2022

- *Screenshot from one girl states "too aubreigh fucking try me" with her face behind the text.*

- *Screenshot of Snapchat message thread as well. One girl called Aubreigh a bitch, telling her that she ruins everything. That all of Aubreigh's friends talk "shit" about her.*

- *Aubreigh sends a screenshot to the mother of the girl and says:*

  "I hate to be a bother, but I feel like I should speak up. I talked to my mom, and she said I should do what I feel is best, and she contacted you as well, but it is very upsetting how she talks about me. I have told her multiple times to please stop, and she doesn't. I am in no means meaning to get her in trouble or tell on her. Just upsetting because this is becoming an everyday thing and we do have a class together." (No response from the mother.)

- *In another thread, Aubreigh asked a girl to stop talking badly about her. The response:*

  "I can say wtv I want 😂 ... I don't talk about everyone. I just talk about you." Aubreigh writes, "why, I didn't do anything." Girl responds simply with "k."

- *Another girl posted mocking TikToks referencing Aubreigh. I contacted her mom, asking her to intervene. Aubreigh also messaged:*

  "Please can you get her to stop. I'm over it. I blocked her on everything to try and stop the drama and she makes these. It's getting out of hand." (No response from the mom.)

2023

- *Another girl sends bullying messages to Aubreigh via social media during school. This girl calls Aubreigh a bitch. Aubreigh tells her to keep her name out of her mouth. The response was, "I'll talk about you all I want, and u ain't shit babe."*

- *Aubreigh texted while at school, "I am so over it. ▆▆▆▆ and ▆▆▆▆ talk crap about me 24/7. I don't even talk to them. I hear them all the time talking about me and pointing at me at lunch. They have no room to talk, and that's all they do. I am truly over it."*

77

- *Aubreigh reports vulgar comments from a boy. The teacher is notified via email, but takes no further administrative action.*

- *I sent one of the girls' fathers screenshots of social media interaction. He responded with concern and said he would speak to his daughter and stop the behavior. The girl sent text messages after her father was notified. We sent the same message to the girl's mom, said she would talk to her daughter and ensure no further contact, and requested that I also provide the same from Aubreigh.*

- *Group chats circulated at school: name-calling, exclusion, mocking. Aubreigh was isolated and targeted repeatedly. Every attempt to report only escalated retaliation. She was labeled a "snitch," making her even more vulnerable.*

- *Aubreigh described constant cruelty in texts, including being mocked at lunch daily, called "fat," and belittled. Screenshots show other students admitting these comments were made.*

- *Two of the girls had her lunch, walked behind her frequently laughing, and snickering behind her back as they mocked her. (In the presence of faculty)*

- *The sexual assault. (Discussed in person)*

- *After she reported being sexually assaulted at a school event, administrators questioned her alone, against my request. The fallout led to students creating "Team Him" vs. "Team Aubreigh." Aubreigh was hit in the face by one of the girls. Notified admin staff.*

- *A student throws a cell phone at Aubreigh, hitting her. I prompted her to tell admin. Out of fear, Aubreigh states she isn't a snitch.*

- *Aubreigh texts that one of the girls is calling her a 'bitch' at school.*

And those were the things I had without even looking deeply; later, I would find more. My soul was shattered for her. The bullying was truly unrelenting. In person, online, in classrooms, at lunch, in group chats. She was targeted, mocked, and physically hurt. Every time she sought help, the system either minimized, ignored, or worsened her situation. Aubreigh carried years of torment, and despite constant reports, nothing changed.

I sat and stared at the computer screen for the longest time. I couldn't get myself to type out the date she died for the timeline. I knew I had to. An attorney would need it. The police had it. I'd never forget the date. But at that moment, I had the hardest time getting it on the page.

I took a break. My head was pounding, and I knew I was about to have a meltdown. I went to the kitchen, filled my water glass, and drank the entire thing in a few gulps. I refilled it and drank the whole glass again. And by the third time I refilled it, I could feel the tears coming. The pressure in my head was so tight. I put the glass down and slide down the cabinets onto the floor. I pressed my head into my hands and let myself fall apart.

I sobbed and screamed. Until I couldn't get anything else out. When I could stand again, I walked over to the laptop I was working on, typed in September 4th, 2023: Died of suicide.

I didn't sleep well that night. I was anxious to meet the attorney and learn about my legal options. *Could I sue those families? Could I sue that school?* Those questions were rolling around in my mind all night. I just wanted accountability. I just wanted them to know what they had done was wrong, that their cruelty had consequences.

My mind spun in circles, replaying every question, every possibility, every "what if." And before I knew it, morning, September 19th had come.

It started like any other day. When the sunshine peeked through the blinds, I pushed my tired body out of bed and went to the kitchen for a cup of coffee. I still had hours before my friend, Kassi, would come to the house. She agreed to accompany me to the attorney's office because I didn't want to take that next step alone. Wanting justice for Aubreigh and going after it would take so much energy, and I needed all the support I could get.

I got Taylor and Ryker up for school, packed their lunches, and got them both out to the door. I drove Ryker to school, but Taylor was able to do what she needed to do to get to school on time.

Later that day, Kassi drove us to the law office. The building itself felt intimidating, the kind of place where the weight of decisions hangs in the air. We were ushered into a large conference room, massive, really, with a long table that looked like it could seat twenty people. Leather chairs lined both sides.

We chose seats close together. One attorney sat at the head of the table, another across from me. I sat beside the head chair, and Kassi was on my right, close enough to feel her steady presence. My hands ached from how tightly I kept them clasped, but I needed her there to remind me I wasn't walking into this alone.

At first, the questions were simple: details about what had happened, what Aubreigh had endured, what I wanted to see change, what protections I needed in place. But then the conversation began to shift. The questions grew heavier, more specific, the kind that cut deeper and demanded rawness and vulnerability.

That's when the attorney paused and explained something I hadn't thought of before. He told us that while I had attorney-client privilege, Kassi did not. He told me that privilege wasn't about guilt or innocence; it was about protection. If I shared details with her in the room, and if she were ever questioned later, she could legally be compelled to repeat what was said. That could backfire, not because I had anything to hide, but because grief is messy, lawsuits are messy, and words can be twisted. He wanted to make sure every single word I spoke in that room was safe and protected. He gently suggested that Kassi step out for the remainder of the meeting.

I didn't fully understand all the legal reasons, but I knew enough to recognize it mattered. I turned to Kassi with gratitude, wishing she could stay but knowing I had to continue on my own. She gave my arm a squeeze, a quiet reminder that I wasn't alone in spirit, even if she couldn't sit beside me in that moment.

When the door closed behind her, the room felt bigger, colder, quieter. Just me and the attorneys now, their eyes steady. The real work was about to begin.

Once it was just me and the attorneys, the real conversation began. Questions were asked—hard ones, necessary ones—and I answered as best as I could through the fog of grief. Out of respect for the fact that this is still an active legal matter, I won't go into detail here. What I can say is that we laid everything on the table: what Aubreigh endured, what I had reported, and what steps might come next.

They explained how the process would begin. Every report, every document, every file from the school and the police station would need to be gathered and examined. Nothing could move forward until that groundwork was done. It was daunting, knowing how much information there was to uncover, but also reassuring to know that it would no longer just sit in silence.

By the time we left, I had signed papers, retaining them to represent the Wyatt family.

I left that room knowing the wheels had begun to turn. Vague though I must be, the truth is this: that day marked the start of accountability, the first steps toward shining light into the places where darkness had lingered far too long.

When we left the law office, I felt wrung out. My body moved on autopilot as Kassi drove us back through familiar streets, but my mind was still trapped in that conference room, replaying every question, every answer, every heavy silence. By the time we pulled into my driveway, I was barely upright.

Kassi hugged me tightly before I stepped inside, her presence a reminder that I wasn't carrying this alone, even if it felt like it. But once I shut the door behind me, the strength I'd been clinging to unraveled. I made it only as far as the couch before collapsing into it, curling up, and finally releasing the grief I had kept pressed down during those long hours across from the attorneys.

The exhaustion wasn't just physical; it was everything. Grief, fear, anger, hope, all tangled together until there was nothing left but tears and silence.

September 20th, 2023

That morning, with barely a moment to gather my thoughts from meeting with the attorney the day before, I found myself walking into yet another room heavy with responsibility. September 20th, 2023. This time, it was with an investigator from the Ocean Springs Police Department. Kassi drove me there, the same steady presence she had been the day before, and she stayed with me through the entire meeting. Just having her beside me at the table gave me the courage to keep answering, even when the questions felt like they were pressing into wounds that hadn't even begun to heal.

The conversation was measured and professional, but I could feel the invisible weight in the room as we went over details. The more the investigator spoke, the tighter the knot in my stomach became.

Aubreigh had been gone for more than two weeks by that point. And, I concluded in that time, the Ocean Springs Police Department didn't care about my daughter's death or why she hung herself. I don't know if it was because they carried a tainted, oversimplified view of suicide, or if they simply didn't want to shoulder the weight of such a case.

Their approach felt dismissive, as if they had already decided it wasn't worth their time. Letting it fade into someone else's jurisdiction or completely disappear was easier. To just let this be another suicide, or to dig for the truth.

Their handling of her phone was one of the clearest examples. The search was so surface-level that they didn't even uncover her second social media account, which could have held critical information. It was sloppy work, lackadaisical, and most devastating. They didn't comb through her messages, contacts, or online activity with the thoroughness such a case demanded. They simply skimmed. And then, as if to underline the apathy, two of the minors involved never even came in to be questioned. They refused to meet or talk, and the police let it go without pressing further. There were no follow-ups, no push for answers, just a quiet passing of the file to youth court, washing their hands of the responsibility. From my perspective, it felt like they did everything they could to check the bare minimum boxes without ever truly investigating. And that was something I would never forget.

The investigator handed Aubreigh's phone back to me and told me that because the children involved were juveniles, the case would have to be handed over to the youth court.

I was stern but polite and left his office when he told me my daughter's case was no longer his concern. Walking to my car, I kept reminding myself that the case wasn't closed yet.

What I wanted was for that investigator to pursue charges against those girls and their families, but instead of pursuing charges, he told me to wait. I didn't want to push too hard, didn't want to risk someone not giving their full effort because I upset them, but it felt like another hurdle in a journey already tangled with obstacles. It was the next step, though, and I had no choice but to take it.

September 21st brought another step forward. I got an email from my attorney letting me know he would send out a press release to the local media, announcing that I had retained legal counsel. He also notified the school district to preserve all relevant letters and records. It was a small but necessary measure of paperwork and procedure that would hold people accountable later.

SEPTEMBER 21st, 2023 PRESS RELEASE

Aubreigh Wyatt's family has recently retained the attorneys of Davis & Crump, P.C. in Gulfport, MS to investigate the circumstances of Aubreigh's tragic death. Though the investigation continues, there is substantial evidence to suggest that bullying and cyberbullying sub-stantially contributed to Aubreigh's death. Honored to represent this family in this time of incomprehensible grief, Davis & Crump will do everything possible to hold accountable those who bullied, harassed, and mistreated this poor child and those who allowed this behavior to occur. Aubreigh's family and Davis & Crump also hope that law enforcement personnel with jurisdiction over this matter will continue to investigate this tragedy, and that justice will be served in the criminal justice system in addition to the civil justice system.

The plague of bullying and cyberbullying is a very real and present threat to our society, especially to our children and youth. If the perpetrators of this type of

senseless and horrific behavior are not held accountable, this plague will continue to devastate our children.
Parents, teachers, and school systems must be vigilant in
preventing bullying. If they are not, they must be held
accountable. Similarly, children must be taught that
bullying hurts, traumatizes, and sometimes even kills
its victims.

If we do not address this problem now, we risk the safety
of all of our children.

The local newspaper picked up the story quickly. On September
25th, the paper had our story on its front page.

The headline read: *Teen's family seeks justice after bullying led
to death.* There was a photo of a woman putting flowers down at a
memorial for Aubreigh. The paper used Aubreigh's class photo. The
article was in-depth and covered a lot of ground. I was grateful for the
attorney speaking on our behalf. He told the reporter as much as he
could without naming the girls, but did say that "one group of students, led by girls, started bullying her when she was in fifth grade."

I read it. I hated reading it. But I did it.

Social media followed. Then, the national media outlets picked up
on the story.

The coverage was constant for weeks; it felt like I was living inside
headlines, my personal tragedy displayed for strangers to read over
their morning coffee. It was a blessing and a curse.

I hoped the news coverage would help her case. But I didn't hear a
word from the youth court or the investigator the rest of the month.
What the media coverage did for us was keep her name at the top of

our minds. I continued to share her images, videos, and pleas for parents to talk to their children about bullying and suicide.

I returned to work the last week of September 2023.

As I was walking in those side doors from my car, I recalled every single morning that Aubreigh would walk in with me, her small steps matching mine as we entered the building together. From elementary school through her last day of 8th grade, she went in with me. Once out of elementary levels, she walked in to catch the transfer bus. Every day for so many years.

But this time was different. This was the first day since she had started school that she wasn't walking beside me. That absence pressed against me like a weight I couldn't set down. The walk in and then to my classroom felt longer, the classroom quieter, because her presence—something that had always been woven into my mornings there was suddenly gone.

As I walked into my classroom, another memory surfaced. One that had happened only a week or so before she passed. Aubreigh had already left to catch the transfer bus, but she suddenly came rushing back through my door, her backpack bouncing against her shoulders.

"Mom, I need a book," she said, out of breath.

"Any kind?" I asked, confused.

"Yes, any kind."

I looked at the shelves and shook my head. "But these are so much lower than your grade level. What do you even need a book for?"

She didn't explain. She just repeated, "I just need a book."

So I said, "You just grab whatever you think you need." And she did. She slipped it into her bag and hurried off to catch the bus.

Later, after she was gone, I would find that same book still tucked inside her backpack. The sight of it stopped me in my tracks. A simple reminder of an ordinary morning turned sacred by loss.

And now, here I was, standing in that very classroom again, trying to return to some kind of normal. But nothing about it felt normal. The memories pressed in from every corner of the room. At first, I told myself it was manageable, but tears came quickly and without warning. Being around little kiddos in that school environment was harder than I could have prepared for. I'd see a blonde girl with hair like Aubreigh's walking down the hallway, and my chest would tighten until I could barely breathe.

The memories of Aubreigh in that school were suffocating. For years, it had been like a second home for both of us, for all of us really. So many memories, though, of Aubreigh as a student, me as a teacher just a few doors away. I knew where she was every second of the day back then: seeing her at lunch, catching glimpses at recess, waving to her in the halls. Now those same halls whispered like ghosts, carrying shadows of her laughter that I could almost still hear.

My classroom itself was the one she had once helped me decorate. I could still see her little hands carefully placing borders on bulletin boards, lining up books until they looked "just right." Walking back into that space wasn't just uncomfortable. It was like stepping into a living scrapbook, where every corner held a memory that both comforted me and crushed me in the same breath.

After the first few days back at work, I found myself slipping into avoidance. I'd duck into my classroom quickly in the mornings, shutting the door behind me before anyone could catch me in the hall. I kept my head down during transitions, choosing empty corridors or waiting until the crowd cleared before walking to the copier or the office. I wasn't okay, and the last thing I wanted was more pitying eyes or hushed tones when I walked by.

The truth was, conversations had become unbearable. Every time someone stopped me, even with the simplest, most well-meaning question, the tears would start before I could even form an answer. "How are you doing?" became the trigger I dreaded most. I wanted to say, *How do you think I'm doing?* But the words stuck in my throat, replaced only by sobs.

And then there was the look in their eyes, the mix of sorrow, fear, and discomfort. I could feel their hearts breaking for me, but I also felt the way their voices softened, the way their steps quickened after the exchange, as if they didn't know how to stay in my pain for long. Each time it chipped at me. Each time it made me want to shrink smaller, to disappear into the walls of my classroom, where no one would ask questions I couldn't answer.

So, I avoided it. I kept conversations short, smiles forced, my distance carefully guarded. It wasn't about being ungrateful for people's care; I knew they meant well. It was about survival. I was holding myself together by a thread, and every "How are you?" pulled at it until I unraveled again.

I imagine it was hard to talk to me. I was a ticking time bomb on top of a dozen cartons of eggs.

One afternoon, I glanced down a hallway and remembered watching her swing her sweet little backpack on. It was a split second and an insignificant moment in life back then. Post September 4th, 2023, every memory I had of her was important. And those little reminders broke me open at all times of the day. Everyone said they understood, and I was given leeway to excuse myself and *put myself back together*.

But really. A few minutes in a bathroom to stuff down memories of my daughter walking down hallways years before will never equate to me being whole again.

Every day was agony, another dagger to the heart. Every hallway reminded me of Aubreigh. Every classroom felt like a weight pressing down on my chest. Every policy, every expectation, every hushed silence about her was like a wound being reopened.

The worst meltdown happened the day I ran out of three-hole-punched paper pages Aubreigh had helped me punch that summer while I was preparing for the school year. We were in my classroom one day in the middle of July, punching the worksheets for me to use with my next students. We had prepared an entire quarter's worth of work. The day I passed out the last page, it felt like a punch to the gut. How had this much time passed... just another cruel reminder that she would never help me again, that she was gone.

By October, it was Bullying Prevention Awareness Month, and I was not quiet about it, just as I had not been quiet about my daughter being bullied and the school district, the very one I worked for, doing the bare minimum to help her. I was under a microscope, and I knew it.

The more I shared online, the more whispers reached me, not from my boss, the principal, but from other employees about the grumblings at the central office, about their dissatisfaction with how public everything was getting, and that the school district was being put in a bad light.

So the singling out and efforts to shut me up began.

After every post I made about raising awareness of what happened to Aubreigh, or speaking to children about how to be kind to others, or the reality of bullying, or the reality of suicide was met with reprimands. I began to get frequently called over to the central office to talk with the superintendent, human resources, and admin.

I was told to stay quiet. I was told to remember that I was still a teacher even outside the classroom. They wanted me to grieve silently, to bury my pain, to stop pointing fingers at the bullies who had tormented my daughter. They wanted my silence more than they wanted accountability.

I didn't listen. I am a mother first.

It didn't matter what I had posted; if it touched on the truth or cast any kind of shadow over the district, they'd find a way to twist it into something unprofessional. Even something as simple as "Be kind to others, you never know what someone is going through," could be twisted into a reprimand. If my words brushed against the truth, even indirectly, they called it unprofessional.

They told me outright that my social media actions made the school look bad, and as an employee of the district, I had an obligation not to tarnish their image.

One administrator even looked at me directly and said, "You are not allowed to take your teacher hat off when you go home."

I sat there stunned, grieving my child, barely surviving each day, and yet they spoke to me as if my primary responsibility was to shield them from bad publicity. They'd sprinkle in a token acknowledgment of my grief, some shallow comment about understanding my sadness, before pivoting right back to my professionalism.

Every conversation was a strategic squeeze, an attempt to corner me into silence. It became clear that their priority wasn't compassion or truth. They want to control the conversation. And me. And they were willing to chip away at me piece by piece to keep me quiet.

By the middle of October 2023, I was a shell walking through the days. Therapy felt like a small, polite room I kept visiting while the rest of my life burned; no amount of talking would stitch her back together. The thought that everyone's life would somehow right itself if I weren't here started to feel less like a flash of pain and more like a steady drumbeat in my head.

One night, with Ryker staying at his dad's and Taylor was out with friends, that drumbeat got loud enough to steer me. I drove out to the cemetery because the only place that felt honest was where she was. A place that used to make me uneasy, cold stones, rows of names, the hush of dark, the cemetery, once intimidating and morbid. Cemetries used to make my skin crawl—strangers' names, stiff air, the hush of the dark—but when Aubreigh's name joined those rows, the fear washed away. The cemetery stopped being a threat and had turned into a room for my child, a sanctuary where fear had no purchase.

The air was cold and close; the ground smelled of wet earth and old flowers. I lay down beside her, the ugly dirt covering my beautiful child, and let the dark take me, the kind of dark that doesn't just hide things but makes them small enough to fit inside your chest. And I questioned if I could keep going. I turned my phone's location off because I didn't want the world to find me; I told myself I was only staying, only resting, only trying to make sense, and as I thought about joining her, begging God to take me, I fell asleep.

I woke hours later in deeper black than before, and the first bright, searing thought was Taylor and Ryker; two small, ordinary lives that would explode into ruin if I walked away. They had been through enough! Shame hit me quicker than grief had that whole year:

How dare I think their lives would be better without me?

How dare I consider leaving them with another unbearable loss?

They would be crushed.

Stupid Heather.

Selfish. Stupid.

The questions weren't rhetorical; they were a slap that forced me up onto my hands and knees, cold and muddy and furious at myself.

I ran to my car and called Taylor on my way home. I had missed messages and phone calls from her, Nick, Kassi, my brother, friends, and Ryker's dad and stepmom. They flooded my screen like lifelines I hadn't realized were still there.

"I'm so sorry, honey. Don't worry. I'm on my way home," I cried to Taylor.

I couldn't understand what she was saying, but I could hear the panic in her voice. She was wailing, so concerned for me.

"I know, T. I'm coming home right now," I cried back into the phone.

I hit the gas and sped home. In that reckless, raw moment, I felt both the weight of how close I had come and the stubborn, terrible love that kept me from crossing that line, the love that would, in time, become the reason to keep trying.

As I pulled into the house, I saw Nick's and my brother's cars. I knew they were worried, and I felt awful. I was moving so fast that I barely remembered to put the car in park when I turned the engine off. I ran inside and grabbed Taylor. I hugged her hard and whispered in her ear.

"I promise you we will get through this side-by-side. I'm so sorry, honey."

Taylor nodded her head, sobbing into my shoulders.

That night, I surrendered the pain I had inside to God and asked for help to keep marching forward.

After that night, I doubled down on therapy, although I didn't think it was working for me. I wanted therapy to take away the pain, the suffocation of my grief. But really, all it felt like it was doing for me was keeping me in a storm of sorrow, barely able to breathe. But I stayed in it, hoping something would happen in my sessions to help me move forward. It never did, though.

The drive for justice helped me stay out of the really dark place. And the realization that if I didn't stay in front of those claiming to investigate on my behalf, I'd never see justice for my daughter.

One morning, before work, I jumped on my laptop while the kids were getting ready for school and emailed my contact at the youth court.

October 19th, 2023

Good morning,

I hope this message finds you well. I am writing to follow up on my daughter's case and inquire about the next steps in the process. Additionally, I would like to express my willingness to offer any assistance that may be required to facilitate a smooth resolution.

I understand that the youth court system operates with utmost care and responsibility, and I deeply appreciate your commitment to ensuring a fair and just outcome.

Also, if there are any ways in which I can be of assistance or support during this process. Whether it's providing relevant documentation, attending meetings, or any other means by which I can contribute to a positive resolution, please consider me willing and available.

Your guidance and insights regarding the next steps in this process would be greatly appreciated, as it will help us prepare and be as ready as possible.

Thank you for your time and attention to this. I eagerly await your response and further direction.

Sincerely,

Heather Wyatt

I checked my email a hundred times throughout the day. Every break I had, I refreshed my personal account. I stared at my phone during lunch, praying I'd hear something back. But nothing. Nothing for more than a week. And then, my phone rang on October 31st, 2023, minutes before the school bell rang, and my classroom would be flooded with kids.

I glanced down at the phone on my desk and my stomach practically lurched out of my body. I was expecting a call from the youth court system. I didn't recognize the number, but it was local, so I picked it up on the second ring.

"Hello," I said quickly and quietly in case there was someone lurking outside my door.

"Ms. Wyatt?"

"Yes."

It was the youth court clerk. She told me the judge over Aubreigh's case wanted to meet with me the next day at 2:00 p.m. My heart raced and my body tingled.

Finally.

I could have screamed and jumped around out of pure excitement. *Finally. FINALLY. I'm getting justice for my baby.*

My mind immediately began racing, trying to arrange the details. I went straight to my principal's office. I explained that I would need to leave early the next day, not for something casual or a personal errand, but because I had to be in youth court. I told my principal as simply as possible: there were legal matters connected to everything happening with Aubreigh, and I couldn't miss it. It wasn't an official leave form or anything like that, just me doing what teachers always have to do when life collides with the classroom: making sure someone could cover my students while I was gone.

I was thankful my last-minute absence wasn't a big deal. I was assured a substitute teacher would be called in, and I left.

The next day, I walked into that courthouse clinging to a fragile thread of hope. I'd been told a week earlier, *"Everything will be good today. You're in good hands."* Those words echoed through my mind as I sat down, expecting at least a sliver of justice. Instead, the judge's words felt like a death blow all over again.

No case.

Because my daughter wasn't alive to testify, the youth court had decided they couldn't do anything, not against the girls who tormented her, not against the boy who sexually assaulted her. Without her physically present to speak the words she had already written down in her witness statement, they claimed their hands were tied, even with solid evidence. Solid proof, it did not matter.

I'd never cried so much or felt so gutted. It was as if the legal system had confirmed what I feared all along, that my daughter's voice, her truth, could be erased simply because she was gone. They said it is a "he said, she said" situation, and since Aubreigh was not here for her part, then it would not matter in court. None of the evidence mattered, none of her statements, none of the reports, or records from the school, the few they did keep up with.

And then came the part that cut even deeper. They told me that even if she were still here, *if she sat in that room and testified,* it would still not result in any type of discipline. There was a one-year statute of limitations for sexual assault (even though we had not yet reached that), and in addition to that, the youth court's job was not to punish but to "rehabilitate and redirect." At most, it would have been nothing more than a redirection. Nothing would change.

I couldn't keep listening. My body shook with rage and grief as I stood up and yelled:

"They will do this again! They will continue to bully, and another child will die because you didn't do anything!"

And then I walked out.

I'd never cried so much or felt so gutted. It was as if the legal system had confirmed what I feared all along, that my daughter's voice, her truth, could be erased simply because she was gone.

The case wasn't officially closed, but local police had already told me they wouldn't pursue anything; it was out of their jurisdiction. And now, the youth court had made it clear they wouldn't take action either, because Aubreigh wasn't here. My next step would be to meet with the district attorney, carrying what little hope I had left.

7

IME SEEMED TO PLAY CRUEL TRICKS ON ME. SOME DAYS FELT like they stretched on for years, the weight of grief making every hour drag, while others vanished in a haze before I could catch my breath.

November 2023 brought on two more firsts for me. It was the first time I was put on administrative leave as a result of continuing to post statements about my daughter being bullied to the point of death.

And it was the first Thanksgiving since Aubreigh's passing—the first real big holiday.

Every year, we took a family vacation together. It didn't always fall on Thanksgiving, but it always happened. That was our tradition. I hadn't had the privilege of vacations growing up, no suitcases packed for adventures, no "where are we going this year?" excitement, so I made a promise to myself that my children would have those experiences. I'd save all year long if I had to, just to make sure they could step outside the bubble of our town, see the world from somewhere else, and build memories together.

This year's vacation was no different in that sense. We had circled dates on the calendar, counted down the weeks, and planned our days carefully so it would overlap with Thanksgiving. It gave us something to look forward to, a little island of joy in the middle of routine life. Even more exciting this year, my brother Jeff, his wife, and the kids' cousins were coming along! Our small family vacations were something we cherished—packed cars, sometimes flew, new hotel rooms, silly inside jokes, the comfort of just being us in a new place.

And this one should have been no different. We had planned it months before Aubreigh passed, mapping out the details and talking about what we'd do together. We had looked forward to it the way we always did, until suddenly, everything was different.

As the date crept closer, I was torn. A part of me wanted to cancel everything, to stay home where I could sink into my grief without having to pretend. The thought of "fun" felt foreign, almost wrong. But the other part of me couldn't bear the idea of taking something else from Taylor and Ryker. They had already lost their sister. I didn't want them to lose this, too.

So, I decided we would go. We'd experience that first big moment like we had everything else thus far.

Preparing for that first big holiday... I knew it was going to break my heart. I kept myself as busy as possible. I decided to tackle all the legalities and tasks that I could, so that while on vacation, I could be completely there. So, I decided to email the district attorney to check in on Aubreigh's file.

She responded right away.

Dear Ms. Wyatt,

Thank you for your email. I will have my paralegal set up a meeting for us.

I felt productive, responsible, and hopeful.

Thank you. I look forward to meeting you as soon as you can.

That afternoon, I left school with a knot in my stomach that no amount of deep breathing could untangle. I had dressed more carefully that morning, wearing professional clothes and ensuring my hair and makeup were done before heading into work. I knew I'd be driving straight to Pascagoula after teaching without a chance to change. Still, as I gathered my things to leave, I caught myself glancing in the mirror, smoothing my hair, adjusting my blouse as though outward neatness could somehow armor me for what lay ahead.

The drive was only about thirty minutes, but it stretched endlessly. My thoughts ran in circles, bouncing between fragile hope and gnawing dread. One minute, I reminded myself of what I had been told a week earlier: "Everything will be good today. You're in good hands." The next minute, doubt came crashing in: What if nothing changes? What if this is just another dismissal?

Halfway there, I realized I had forgotten to bring a notebook and pen. My heart sank. I've always been a note-taker. It's how I make sense of chaos and ground myself when the world feels overwhelming. Without it, I felt exposed, unprepared. So I pulled into a small store off the highway and hurried inside. The fluorescent lights buzzed above me, and I stood in line clutching a cheap spiral notebook and a pack of pens, almost like they were lifelines. At least I'll have something solid to hold onto, I thought.

I was back in the car within minutes. My stomach was knotted up with anxiety. The steering wheel felt slick under my palms from how tightly I gripped it, and my knuckles were pale with tension. I prayed the entire way, whispering prayers that the truth would matter and that justice would not slip through our fingers again.

I parked in the first open spot outside the office and rushed inside.

The waiting area was dim, lit only by the slant of late afternoon sun through narrow windows. I sat downstairs for a few minutes, knees bouncing, notebook balanced on my lap, pen tapping nervously against the cover. Every sound seemed amplified: the squeak of a chair, the faint hum of a copier down the hall, the rush of blood pounding in my ears.

At last, I was called back. I followed down a narrow hallway and up a staircase that wound and twisted with sharp turns. The stairs clanked underfoot, each step echoing with a metallic groan. My hand brushed the cool metal railing, and I remember thinking how cold it felt against my sweaty palm.

When we reached her office, I felt its weight immediately. The room was quiet but heavy, as if every case, every brokenhearted parent who had ever sat there still lingered in the air: a large brown desk anchored the space, papers stacked neatly to one side. A long table stretched across the room, and I sat down, carefully setting down my brand-new notebook and pen like they might steady me. Her paralegal sat off to the side, silent but watchful.

She greeted me kindly, her voice carrying a softness that made me feel, for a moment, like maybe I could exhale. But the kindness in her eyes did not soften the blow of her words. She told me, carefully and compassionately, that she could do nothing criminally or legally because of outdated laws in Mississippi.

She hated it. She told me she thought it was awful, that the laws were wrong, but her hands were tied.

She pulled out thick law books and flipped through them, the dry rustle of pages filling the quiet. She pointed to statutes line by line, explaining what each one meant, her finger tracing the printed words. She referenced cases, some from Mississippi, others from different states. Each out-of-state case was like salt in the wound, proof that in other jurisdictions there were stronger protections,

protections that might have helped my daughter, but none of them applied here.

She walked me through scenarios, "If this had happened under this law... if she had been this age... if the statute covered this particular type of conduct..." each one ending the same way. Here in Mississippi, nothing could be done for Aubreigh under our outdated laws. She admitted that the same would be true for any other child in a similar situation, especially at that age.

I tried to keep my pen moving, scratching notes across the page, but tears blurred the ink. My chest tightened, my heartbeat loud in my ears.

Her voice softened as she looked at me and said, "Her justice will have to come from God."

Aubreigh would be made whole again through God, through Christ, and nothing could take that from her. Her words landed like both a balm and a blow. They carried faith, yes, but also the sting of finality.

In that moment, hope slipped away, replaced by the familiar sting of dismissal. Once again, the people who were supposed to protect my daughter were telling me there was nothing they could do.

Then she shifted, speaking with conviction. What we could do on earth, she said, was work to change the laws, to update them, to make sure no other child, no other mother, had to sit in this chair and hear that their daughter's pain didn't fit neatly into the legal code.

And with that realization came a fire. If earthly justice could not reach her, then earthly change had to. This was not going to stop on its own. Children would continue to suffer, to be dismissed, to be silenced, unless someone stood up and refused to accept it any longer.

We could try to push for legislative change and fight for new laws that would protect children in the future, but even if those laws were passed, they would not be retroactive and would never affect Aubreigh's case.

The reality hit me with crushing clarity: my baby might never see justice on Earth. Not in the way I had prayed for, not in the way I had fought for. The people who had hurt her could walk away untouched. But Heaven was her court now, and God was the Judge.

The case remained open, which gave me hope. I left that office realizing my fight was more about making sure no other mother would ever sit where I was sitting, being told there was *nothing* the law could do.

> In April 2024, I would learn that keeping her case open was just a technicality. Every non-accidental, unnatural death, including suicides, is presented to the grand jury. There was no pending criminal case. No criminal charges to pursue. It was a process that would move forward for the record, but not for justice.

I walked out of that office numb, carrying both the weight of what I'd heard and the ache of knowing justice might never come in the way I longed for.

I slipped into the rhythm of my classroom for a few days before Thanksgiving break. The halls felt heavy, the same walls that had once echoed with Aubreigh's footsteps now pressing in on me with silence. But routine, even painful routine, gave me somewhere to place my body when my soul felt unmoored.

Thanksgiving Break 2023

And suddenly, it was time for the trip to the Great Wolf Lodge.

We were meeting my brother and his family in North Carolina. It would be our first flight without Aubreigh, our first vacation without Aubreigh.

The morning we left, the air felt heavier somehow. The sky over Ocean Springs was a flat, gray blanket, and the November air had that chill that seeps into your bones before sunrise. I loaded the suitcases into the car, each one lighter than it should have been, not because we packed less, but because one bag was missing. Really, if I am being honest, several. Aubreigh would have overpacked, per usual.

We drove to the New Orleans airport in near silence. Ryker was quietly watching cartoons on his tablet. Taylor had her earbuds in, staring out the window. And me? I kept my eyes on the road, blinking back tears that threatened to spill with every mile.

At the airport, I went through the motions. Though I could have used some time to have a gigantic meltdown, I kept myself together.

I parked, unloaded our bags, and marched us right up to the ticket counter. I gave the agent my name, and she scanned our boarding passes from my phone, three of them. But my chest tightened when I remembered the last time we flew, there were four. I could see her boarding pass, her name printed out.

Security was a blur: shoes off, jackets in bins, laptops out. The conveyor belt's hum and the scanner's sharp beep seemed louder than usual. When we reached our gate, we found a row of seats and dropped our bags. I looked out the expansive glass windows at the runway, watching planes taxi and lift into the sky, and I couldn't stop thinking about how she would have been buzzing with excitement, probably already making TikToks or snapping pictures of her Starbucks cup with her name spelled wrong, as everyone always did!

Boarding was called, and we lined up. I felt the weight of my phone, which had our boarding passes pulled up so that they could be scanned, the finality of walking down that narrow jet bridge without her.

We found our seats, three together. We never got to do that before that trip. It was usually Aubreigh and Taylor in the row ahead, with

Ryker and me behind. I never booked three together, because I didn't want one of them to have to sit alone. I always left a space so it could be two-and-two.

But not that time. That time it was just the three of us. But truthfully, I always felt her presence around us. She was there in spirit. I knew that. I helped Ryker with his seatbelt and watched Taylor settle in by the window, her gaze fixed on the wing. The wing that she and Aubreigh ALWAYS fought about. I would have to delegate rules and say, "One of you gets the wing on the way there, and one of you gets the wing on the way back." But from that point going forward, Taylor could always get the wing. I wondered if that crossed Taylor's mind.

All those arguments about who got the wing, who got the front seat, who would get this or that finally hit me like a ton of bricks as we sat there waiting to take off. Taylor would not have to fight about any of that going forward. Just then, she turned to look at me, and I could see it in her face. There was pain there. I'm sure she could see it in my face, too. I knew she would have given up every wing seat, every shotgun seat, all the first just to have Aubreigh back.

As we took off, the engines roared, and my stomach dropped with the familiar lift. The city fell away beneath us, and the expanse of sky opened up. Usually, flying had always felt like an adventure, like the start of something fun. But this time, every mile between New Orleans and North Carolina felt like a mile further from the life we used to have.

The flight was just under two hours, but it felt longer. I watched the seatbelt sign click off, watched flight attendants roll carts down the aisle, and I kept thinking how Aubreigh would have been nudging Taylor, asking for a Dr. Pepper and a snack, telling her to move so she could go pee. Instead, there was only silence between us, broken by the occasional question from Ryker or a glance from Taylor that said more than words could.

When we landed, the pilot's voice came over the intercom, welcoming us to North Carolina, and my heart ached at the thought of "welcome" without her. We gathered our things, shuffled off the plane, and made our way through the terminal.

Baggage claim was its usual chaos, families crowding around the carousel, kids climbing on suitcases, the clunk and whir of the belt starting up.

The drive to Great Wolf Lodge was just over an hour, but it stretched endlessly in my mind. The closer we got, the tighter my chest became. The last time we planned this trip, Aubreigh was with us, chattering about what rides we'd do first, how late we'd stay in the water park, and which nights we'd sneak out for ice cream. Her voice used to fill the car, her excitement spilling out in a dozen little plans. Now there was only the hum of the road and the suffocating silence of what was missing.

When we arrived, we parked, grabbed our bags, and walked into the warm, wood-paneled lobby. It was already dressed for Christmas. In November, the place transforms into a wonderland—garlands strung across wooden beams, twinkling lights tucked into every corner. The smell of chlorine mixed with the scent of pine and cinnamon drifted through the warm, wood-paneled lobby of the water park, mingled with the sweet scent of cinnamon sugar from the café. Families bustled around us—kids with damp hair and wolf ears, parents juggling room keys and maps. It should have been magical, but for me, it felt like stepping into another life I no longer belonged to.

I knew how much Aubreigh would have loved it. She would have been twirling under the lights, tugging at my arm to see every wreath, every snowflake ornament, sneaking candy canes from the café, laughing with her brother. I could almost see her there. The beauty of it all only made her absence louder.

At the desk, when the clerk handed me our passes and bracelets, there were four. Four—because I had booked the trip for four. And that's when the dam broke. My hand shook as I held the extra bracelet, its plastic band digging into my palm like it carried the weight of the world. That one, single bracelet made it undeniable: she wasn't here. She should've been.

I couldn't move. But somehow my legs carried me. I turned, walked back to the car, and sat there staring at that bracelet until my vision blurred. I cried so hard I couldn't catch my breath, sobs ripping out of me like something primal, something a mother should never have to release. This wasn't the vacation I had planned. I didn't want to be here without her. I didn't want to keep breathing without her.

Eventually, I wiped my face, forced myself to regroup, and hugged my babies tighter than ever. We carried our bags upstairs and made our way to the room.

We were all together in one room, clinging to whatever closeness we could. The days that followed were a blur of laughter and heartbreak. We tried to make the best of it, swimming, sliding, wandering the lodge, but the ache was constant. Ryker played with his cousins, but Taylor, ten years older than most of the kids, as she was the oldest cousin, drifted between trying to join in and sitting quietly on her own.

I could see her looking at other sisters and wishing it were her and Aubreigh, running around, making TikToks, laughing in their own little world. If Aubreigh had been here, between their silly sibling arguments, they would have been inseparable running the halls together, going down water slides, staying up late whispering and giggling, making TikToks and silly dances. I could see it so clearly in my mind that it almost felt real.

I could see how Taylor looked at other sisters and how her eyes followed them when they walked past, laughing. I could feel the unspoken wish that it was her and Aubreigh. She kept her face strong, refusing to let her sadness spill out, but I could see through it. I knew she was breaking inside. She kept her face strong, but I knew she was breaking inside.

When we went to the water park, Taylor didn't have her sister to ride down the slides with or anyone her age to wander the lodge with. I tried to be her partner as much as I could, while Ryker had his cousins to play with. But the truth was, there was a missing piece, and no amount of effort could hide that. One of the hardest parts of grief as a parent is not just holding yourself together, but holding it together for your children.

We continued on, though. We wandered through the lodge, doing the things families do there. Ryker tried his hand at MagiQuest, running through the halls with a plastic wand, chasing lights and treasure like the other kids. We walked past the arcade and the little bowling alley, where the crash of pins and bursts of laughter filled the air. There was mini golf, laser tag, digging for gold, story time in the lobby with kids in pajamas, and restaurants where the smell of pizza and cinnamon sugar lingered in the air. Families filled every corner, moms snapping pictures, siblings laughing until their faces turned red.

It should have been the kind of trip where I just sat back, watched them run free, and breathed in their joy. But the ache was constant. Every time I saw a girl around Aubreigh's age. I had to swallow the lump in my throat. Every time I saw a family with teen daughters, or sisters and little brothers interacting, my eyes stung.

She should have been here.

As our trip came to a close, we knew we wanted to do something special to honor Aubreigh. Aubreigh had always written quotes and

scriptures to herself on Post-it notes and index cards. They were little reminders of hope and truth. Index cards slipped into the frame
of the mirror in her bedroom. Post-it notes tucked into books, into
drawers, on her dresser. We didn't realize just how many there were
until after she passed. Scripture verses, quotes, words of encouragement in her handwriting, simple, ordinary things that became sacred
once we found them. They weren't goodbye notes. They were life
notes, the way she reminded herself to keep going.

When a few people in our town heard about it, they quietly began
doing the same. We never really knew who started it, but all over
Ocean Springs, notecards began appearing in public places—left
on Walmart shelves, tucked into library books, slipped onto coffee shop tables. What Aubreigh had once done privately for herself,
others now did publicly, in her honor. Each note carried the same
kind of encouragement she used to write, many of them signed with
#LiveLikeAubreigh or *#LLA*. It became a ripple effect of kindness, her
way of planting hope now multiplying through the community.

Before we left for our Thanksgiving trip, we invited anyone who
wanted to participate to write notecards or Post-its for us to carry with
us. People dropped them off, handed them to us, sent stacks of them
covered in scriptures and uplifting words. We packed them carefully,
determined that wherever we went, Aubreigh's light would go too.

So on our last day at Great Wolf Lodge, we carried that tradition
forward. We walked the halls together, carrying that little stack of
cards like they were treasure. We slipped them into corners and brochures in the lobby, tucked them into menus at the café, and slid
them between salt and pepper shakers in the restaurants. We left them
at the arcade counters, on bowling alley seats, inside elevators, and
at the bases of the MagiQuest stations where kids waved their wands.
We tucked them behind the room number placards, another onto a
shelf in the gift shop, and left one folded neatly on a pool chair. It

was almost like setting up a scavenger hunt, tiny bursts of encouragement planted all over the lodge, waiting to be discovered.

I imagined some exhausted mom finding one tucked under her
coffee cup, or a little kid tugging at his dad's sleeve to show him a card
that read "You are loved," or a teenager stuffing one into her pocket
after reading a scripture she needed in that exact moment. Maybe
nobody would ever find them. Or maybe the right card would land in
the right hands at the right time.

It was our way of refusing to let the trip end without Aubreigh
leaving her mark here, too. She wasn't physically with us, but her
spirit was scattered through that lodge, folded into every note, hidden
in every corner, planted like seeds of hope we prayed would bloom for
someone else.

When our trip finally came to an end, Thanksgiving break was
over, and it was time to fly home. The thought of leaving was almost
as bittersweet as arriving had been, another flight without Aubreigh,
another "first" we never wanted to have.

When the last card had been tucked away and the last corner
searched, reality set back in. It was time to pack our bags, gather up
the wet swimsuits and wolf ears, and face the end of Thanksgiving
break. The lobby that had felt so magical when we first arrived now
felt heavy, like we were carrying both memories and absence out the
door with us. A new memory that didn't hold Aubreigh.

The thought of leaving was almost as bittersweet as arriving had
been, another flight without Aubreigh, another "first" we never
wanted to have. But before I could even linger in that grief, life, as
it so often does, demanded my full attention. Ryker had suddenly
come down with an awful illness. It hit hard and fast, and by the time
we reached the airport, all my energy was poured into caring for him,
making sure he was comforted, making sure we just got home.

At the airport, it became painfully clear just how sick he was. I remember looking over and seeing him lying flat on the floor in the terminal, too weak to sit upright, too miserable to care about the noise or the people walking around us. My heart broke in a whole different way. All I could think was: *Just let me get my baby home.*

There was no time to dwell on grief, no space for the ache of missing her in that moment. My focus narrowed completely to get him home safe and get him to a doctor. I tried everything I could think of: medicine, water, snacks, even just holding him against me, but nothing stayed down. His little body was wearing out from the constant vomiting. The signs of dehydration were creeping in, and I could feel the urgency pressing down on me with every passing minute. For a while there, I thought maybe I should rent a car and just drive home, but I knew that would take even longer.

Taylor and I did all we could to comfort him on the flight, keeping him warm, holding his hand, whispering reassurances. She rubbed his back while I held a bag for him to be sick in, both of us working wordlessly together because we knew we had one mission: get him home.

When we finally landed in New Orleans, I moved like a machine— bags gathered, kids in tow, pushing us through the airport and into the car. We got home late, and that night we collapsed into bed, wrung out and empty.

The next morning, I was back in "mom mode." First urgent care, then the ER, searching for answers as Ryker's little body fought against a brutal virus. It was miserable to watch, but eventually the doctors settled on rotavirus—likely something he'd picked up in the chaos of travel. Slowly, painfully, he began to mend.

It struck me in those days how relentless life can be. One moment, I was drowning in grief, the next I was in a fluorescent-lit ER, holding a sick child, shifting into fight-mode because that's what motherhood demands. There's no pause button for sorrow. No space to collapse the way you want to. It's always go, go, go.

A few days later, Thanksgiving break was over, and school had started back. The trip that had been months in the making, planned with excitement, taken in grief, and ended in illness was now just another chapter in the year that had changed everything. Routine picked back up. We were back in school, Buses rolled, bells rang, and classrooms filled again as if nothing had happened. But for me, nothing was normal. Grief followed me into every hallway, and my posts online about bullying, bringing awareness, sharing my grief, sharing who my daughter was, suicide awareness, and Aubreigh's story followed me into the workplace.

By November 30th, just a few days after returning, I was placed on administrative leave. They called it "investigating my posts" and checking whether I had violated rules or regulations as a teacher of the district. But I knew what it was, an attempt to silence me, to scare me into submission. To dangle my job over my head, knowing I was a single mom whose income fed her children. It was never about professionalism. It was about control.

Within those five days on leave, the quiet gave me no relief. Instead, it forced me to face questions I had been shoving aside just to survive. Was this really what was best for me? Was this job worth the cost to my mental health? Could I keep walking into those halls, knowing what I knew, feeling what I felt, being told to shut up about the very thing that took my daughter?

The back-and-forth was relentless. One moment, I was terrified of losing the job that kept food on the table and bills paid. The next, I wondered if holding on was costing me more than it was giving me. I had already lost my child. I was drowning in grief, and now the people I worked for dangled my livelihood over my head as if my silence was more valuable than my pain.

It was a tug-of-war I couldn't win. Grief yanked me one way, fear the other. Anger surged, then gave way to despair. I would sit and think, *How do I keep doing this?* Then I'd snap back with the reminder, *You don't have a choice. You have kids who depend on you.* It was a mental loop that never stopped, every thought colliding with the next until I could barely breathe.

Three months earlier, my entire world had shattered. And here I was, not even out of the first season of grief, already being tested, already being cornered, already being told that my voice was a problem. It was too much. The weight of it pressed down on me.

In that time, I finally decided to pull back from social media. I had poured myself into posting, advocating, and speaking out about bullying, suicide, and Aubreigh's story. At first, it felt like purpose, like a way to fight back against the silence I had been pushed into. Every post left me wide open for scrutiny, for criticism, for judgment from the very people who should have been standing beside me. For the sake of my own mental health, I logged off, knowing it would be temporary, but it was for my sanity, my peace of mind. I didn't stop caring. I didn't stop believing in the need for change. I just knew that at that moment, I couldn't carry both the weight of my grief and the constant fight with the district that was determined to silence me.

By the end of those five days, I was called back into a meeting. I braced myself for the worst, but instead, the message was simple: "You can return to work." That was it. Nothing more. All of their "concerns," all the supposed investigations into whether I had broken rules or regulations, led to nothing. No findings. No consequences. No apology. Just a cold green light to return, as if the whole ordeal had been nothing more than a scare tactic. It confirmed what I had known deep down: this was never about professionalism. It was about control. About reminding me that they could hold my job, and therefore my livelihood, over my head whenever they chose.

When I returned, it was already early December. Only about two weeks until Christmas break. On paper, it should have felt manage-able—just hold it together until the holidays, then exhale. But grief doesn't care about calendars. And the holidays don't soften grief; they sharpen it. Every Christmas light, every song on the radio, every decoration felt like another knife twisting.

Walking back into school, I was already depleted. My body moved, but my heart wasn't in it. My mind raced with the what-ifs—what if I couldn't keep this up, what if I broke down in front of a class, what if I lost my job entirely? At the same time, another voice whispered that maybe losing it wouldn't be the worst thing, because how could I keep showing up in a place that wanted me silent about the very thing that killed my daughter?

December has always been a season of anticipation, of joy. But that year, it felt like a looming storm cloud. I felt dread more than excite-ment. The world sparkled with holiday magic, but inside, all I could feel was doom pressing down. The ache of knowing this would be the first Christmas without Aubreigh seeped into everything. There was no escaping it. Not at home, not at school, not in my own head. And still, somehow, I was expected to smile, to teach, to carry on as if I wasn't breaking apart piece by piece.

I was worn down mentally, emotionally, and physically. My own grief sat like an anchor in my chest, but I was also carrying Taylor and Ryker's grief. Their heartbreak didn't look exactly like mine, but I could feel it in the air, see it in their faces, hear it in the quiet moments when they didn't know I was listening. Parenting while grieving is its own kind of impossible—you're asked to be the steady ground when all you want is to collapse.

And then there was the other weight: the never-ending tension with the school district. The constant reprimands. The administrative leave. The meetings felt less like support and more like interrogations. On top of that were the legal battles, meeting with investigators, sitting in the district attorney's office, meeting with youth court officials, all crammed into just a few short months.

It had taken everything out of me. I felt hollow, like I had nothing left to give to my job, my kids, even myself. I knew I wasn't healing. I wasn't even moving in a direction that looked like healing. That's when I decided I'd push through until Christmas break, take the two weeks off, and then reevaluate. If I still felt this way, I'd go back out on medical leave. I wasn't good for myself, much less for a classroom of 25 eight-year-olds.

But even as I made that promise to myself, I knew Christmas would be its own breaking point. Our first Christmas without Aubreigh. A milestone I had dreaded since the day she left us.

The weeks leading up to break were a strange mix of numb and raw. I took things one small piece at a time, just focusing on getting through each school day, one errand, one chore at a time, but the heaviness was always there. It would sneak up on me in moments I didn't expect: scrolling online and realizing I wasn't buying her anything this year, overhearing kids talk about what they'd asked for, remembering how she would have been sending me her shopping list.

Aubreigh didn't just make a Christmas list; she turned it into a full-scale multimedia presentation. One year, she built an entire PowerPoint, slide by slide, each one dedicated to a category: shoes, tops, bottoms, purses, perfume, makeup. If it were shoes, she'd give me three or four carefully curated options, complete with pictures. And these weren't just for browsing pleasure; every single image was hyperlinked directly to the website, with her preferred size, color, and style already picked out.

It was part-shopping list, part-scavenger hunt, part-tech genius at work. All I had to do was click and buy. She was her own personal stylist and Santa's logistical coordinator in one.

Another year, she leveled up to an Amazon Wish List. It was the same concept, but even more streamlined. Whenever someone asks, "What do you want for Christmas?" she didn't rattle off ideas. She'd just send them the link—one click, problem solved.

It was so her, organized, polished, and just the tiniest bit extra in the best way possible. She wasn't just asking for gifts; she was delivering a whole experience. That mix of perfectionism, humor, and efficiency? That was pure Aubreigh.

But that year... there was no list. No links. No texts popping up on my phone at midnight with, "Mom, look at this!"...

Usually, Christmas shopping for me was always part-military operation, part-math exam, and part-magic trick. Every year, I'd start with a set budget, usually a teacher's salary version of "the sky's the limit," and somehow divide it equally between three kids. And not just equal in money, but equal in gift count, too. Because nothing says "Merry Christmas" like two children tearing into their fourth present while one sits there staring at a lone sweater.

I'd be in the middle of Target, the calculator app open, muttering to myself like a Wall Street broker on the verge of a breakdown. "Okay, if Taylor gets the AirPods, then Aubreigh gets the shoes, and Ryker gets the Switch game... but that's $18 more for Ryker, so I need to find something $18-ish for the girls, or it's war."

That's the unwritten mom code, especially for single moms on a tight budget: keep it fair, keep it balanced, keep the peace. I wanted them to have everything possible, get the best life, but equally.

But that year... I only had two kids to shop for.

And instead of feeling like I had more money to spread around, it gutted me. The silence of not having to calculate her column, not needing to count her gifts, not clicking through her hyperlinks, was deafening. My cart felt heavier than ever, not with gifts, but with the reality of the empty space in my list, and in my life.

There was no list from her this year. No clever presentations. No last-minute requests. Nothing she needed, because she wasn't here to need it. That truth hit me over and over, like a fresh wound every single time.

It is a particular kind of agony that only a mother can understand: standing in the middle of a store at Christmas and realizing one of your babies has nothing under the tree because she will never again sit there to open it. Your hands go through the motions, grabbing gifts, scanning prices, keeping up appearances, but your heart is screaming. Everything inside of you wants to throw the cart aside, collapse onto the cold tile, and scream at the world that this isn't fair, that she should be here.

And yet, you keep moving. Because that's what motherhood demands. Because Taylor and Ryker still needed Christmas. Because you're not allowed to quit, even when all you want is to freeze time at the last holiday where your family was whole.

But nothing about this year felt whole.

That empty space followed me everywhere. When it came time to decorate, part of me wanted to skip it entirely. Aubreigh always helped. She was my decorator, my artist, my one with a vision. Once again, I did not want to take any more away from Taylor or Ryker, though, so even though it gutted me, even though it hurt like hell, even though every single decoration was a reminder of my child that was forever gone, I decided to decorate.

Decorating for Christmas was always an event in our home, a slow, deliberate layering of magic. First came the trees, laughter and joy filling the air as we fluffed branches and untangled strings of lights. We always put on the movie " The Santa Clause" while drinking hot cocoa. Then, little by little, we transformed the house. A wreath on the front door, garland draped everywhere, snow globes nestled into corners where they could catch the light.

I set up our main Christmas tree in the living room, my "perfect" tree. I'll admit it: I'm obsessive about that one. The lights are evenly spaced, the ribbon just so, every ornament placed intentionally. It's the picture-perfect tree with red and gold decorations, balanced and beautiful.

But the real heart of our Christmas decorations was always the "kid tree" in the dining room. That tree wasn't about perfection; it was about memories. It held every ornament the kids had ever made: popsicle-stick frames with preschool pictures, lopsided paper angels, little clay handprints from kindergarten. And every year, since Taylor was a baby, then Aubreigh, and then Ryker, I had given each child their own ornament, something they picked out themselves that reflected their personality and interests that year.

There was the year we did Disney, and all the ornaments were different characters. There was Taylor's first favorite cartoon, Elmo, taking a spot of honor. Aubreigh's ornaments sparkled with her personality. Her very first, a tiny pink and white baby shoe, then Elsa, a ballerina, a butterfly, each one capturing the color and brightness she carried into every room. Taylor's later years leaned into her teen style: soccer players, a hoodie, and little pieces of who she was becoming. Ryker's were still fresh and few: his first baby ornament, an elephant, a silhouette, then the beginnings of his sports, football and baseball players. Each one proudly marked with their name and year.

That December, putting up the kid tree was one of the hardest things I've ever done. Every ornament of hers was a punch to the chest, a memory frozen in time. I could see her little hands carefully placing them, hear her voice reminding me which branch they *had* to go on, the way she'd tilt her head to make sure it was just right. This year, there was no new ornament for her to choose. Taylor and Ryker still picked theirs, and we had one customized for Aubreigh with all her favorite things. But the process didn't feel magical; it felt heavy, weighted with absence.

Still, we kept going. One ornament after another, one step forward, even when it felt impossible. That's the thing about grief: you don't really get a choice. You keep breathing, keep moving, keep putting one foot in front of the other, even when your heart is splintering with every touch of glass and ribbon.

And when the ornaments were hung and the tree stood finished, another tradition was waiting. The one that was just ours. One of my favorite parts of Christmas, the one that belonged to Aubreigh and me alone, was building our snow village. It had started a few years earlier, a quiet idea we shared one December evening, and since then, each year we added something new. A tiny café with frosted windows, a cozy little cottage, a couple ice-skating in the town square, Santa with his sleigh, even a snowboarder frozen mid-jump. Every piece was chosen carefully, our collection growing slowly each year.

That year, though, the air felt heavier as I unpacked the boxes. My hands hovered over the familiar figurines, my heart splintering. This was ours. Our thing. And now, half of that "us" was missing. A part of me wanted to smash it all into pieces, to end the tradition because it hurt too much. But another part of me clung to it, desperate to keep it alive, maybe as a way of keeping her alive, too.

So I went to the store, as I always had, to see what new treasure I could find. And there it was. A large carousel, spinning gracefully, its platform dotted with tiny villagers in winter coats. I froze. Last year, Aubreigh had begged for it, her eyes lit with that mix of hope and mischief she always had when she wanted something. But we couldn't get it then. We had already picked out so many new additions to the snow village. I'd promised her we would the next year.

Now, here it was, alone, literally the only one left, perched on the highest shelf like it had been waiting for me. I had to climb halfway up the display just to reach it, my fingertips brushing its box. When I finally pulled it down and held it close, I knew. This wasn't just another piece for the snow village. This was Aubreigh's piece. This was meant to be. And so I brought it home and placed it right in the heart of our little town, where it could spin forever.

The night before Christmas, we had tried to keep all of our traditions, and this one was no different: cookies and milk for Santa, hot cocoa for us, and sitting together in our matching pajamas, but even the warmth of those rituals felt muted.

And then came Christmas morning. That first Christmas without her. Waking up felt like being split in two, part of me forcing my body to move through the motions, the other part screaming inside that she should be here. The silence before the kids woke up was unbearable. No soft footsteps padding down the hall. No whispered excitement from her voice, asking if it was time yet. Just an emptiness that swallowed the room whole.

Every mother knows the magic of Christmas morning—the way your children's faces light up, the squeals echoing through the house, the laughter that bubbles out with every torn piece of wrapping paper. But that morning, for me, it wasn't magic. It was a crushing weight. The ache of one child missing. The stockings were hung, but hers stayed still. The presents were wrapped, but none had her name on them. Even before a single gift was touched, the absence screamed louder than anything else in the room.

As we walked into the living room, I forced myself to do what I always did—I slid cinnamon rolls onto a pan, the smell of cinnamon sugar and dough meant to fill the air with warmth. But even as the oven ticked and hummed, the sweetness was hollow. We smiled. We laughed. The kids unwrapped with wide eyes. And yet, beneath it all, there was a constant ache, sharp and unrelenting.

Usually, Christmas mornings alternated with Ryker's dad, one year with me, the next with him. But December 2023 was different. He knew. He knew this Christmas couldn't be split, not when it was our first without her. He told me to keep Ryker, and it was a mercy I'll always be grateful for. We were all together, and yet... not whole.

However, even with all of us together, Christmas morning felt different. The usual flow of opening gifts was one child at a time, gift by gift. I could snap a picture, and they could soak in their joy without the chaos of everyone tearing into paper all at once. Taking turns so the morning lasted, and round we'd go, me pulling one from under the tree and passing it out, making sure each gift had its own little spotlight. This year, the rhythm was broken. There was no one to fill that space between Ryker and Taylor. The unwrapping went faster, and it felt emptier.

When it came time for stockings, hers hung there like it always did, but I couldn't bring myself to fill it with candy or small gifts. Instead, we placed flowers in it, the ones we would take to her gravesite later that day.

Over the years, the stockings have become the main event. I don't even know exactly when it happened, but at some point, they outshone the actual presents under the tree.

Inside those stockings were the "*good* things," the gift cards, the makeup, the fancy hairbrush, the trendy little accessories you'd been eyeing but never bought for yourself. Basically, all the stylish, coveted items that made you light up. And honestly? Anything I thought was too small or awkward to wrap ended up in there, too.

Of course, tradition was tradition, so they always got the annual "replenish" items, fresh socks, undergarments, a new toothbrush, and toothpaste because I'm still a mom. But between those practical things were all the tiny treasures, gadgets, and trinkets that made you feel like you'd just hit the jackpot.

It was like Mary Poppins' bag in stocking form. You'd pull one thing out, and there was still more waiting at the bottom.

In our house, stockings weren't just part of Christmas morning; they were the real grand finale or the opening act, depending on how you looked at it.

Every Christmas morning, Taylor and Aubreigh had this unspoken tradition of waking up long before I did. I'd still be tucked under the covers when they tiptoe out to the living room, giggling softly, their socks sliding on the floor as they made a beeline for the stockings.

I could practically picture it without even being there. They whispered, "Look at this!" as they pulled out treasures one by one. The stockings were like treasure chests, overflowing with makeup palettes, fuzzy socks, hair accessories, tiny perfumes, gift cards, and all the little luxuries they loved.

Then, after their secret raid, they'd tiptoe back to my room, eyes wide and voices bright, shaking me awake with that breathless, Christmas-morning urgency pretending they hadn't already rifled through every last item. I'd always play along, letting them keep their little sisterly secret. But inside, I'd be smirking, because I knew. I always knew. And honestly? I loved it. That quiet, early-morning ritual was as much a part of our Christmas as the stockings themselves.

So Christmas morning began, every part of Christmas was still there: the decorations, the food, the gifts, the routines, but without her, none of it felt complete. There was a gap in everything, a missing note in every song. I tried to hold it together for Taylor and Ryker, to make sure they felt some joy that morning, but inside, I knew this was only the beginning of all the "firsts" we would face without Aubreigh.

The rest of Christmas break unfolded in quiet fragments. We visited her gravesite, placing the flowers from her stocking gently on top of where she lay. They looked so small there, delicate against the earth. I whispered *Merry Christmas* through tears.

2023 was the year I lost my daughter. The year my family was shattered. The year grief carved itself into every part of my being. And no matter how many calendars turned, no matter how many fireworks lit the sky, there would never be a "new year" that undid that.

8

The Aubreigh Wyatt Foundation

Somehow, I made it through 2023, and not because I felt strong, but because I didn't have a choice. I had two children still here who needed me, and a God who somehow kept carrying me, one breath at a time.

So 2024 came, ready or not.

We stepped back into the school building the first week of January. Returning from Christmas break to classrooms and to something I hadn't had the space to reconcile yet: my pain. Maybe routine would help. Maybe structure would keep me steady. But it didn't take long, less than a week, for me to see clearly that I couldn't stay.

Within a matter of days of a brand new year, and what would be the start of the first full year without Aubreigh, I learned the school wasn't interested in including her in her middle school yearbook.

I knew the elementary school was sending out emails to us teachers to upload photos for the yearbook. While it seemed early. Typically, the yearbook photos needed to be finished by February. So I knew we were finalizing their yearbook for our students.

I began to wonder what would happen with Aubreigh's. She hadn't been able to purchase one, and she hadn't taken a school picture that fall. I was curious what they would use for her photo, and since it was customary for the school to create a dedication page when a student passed, I assumed something similar would be in the works for my daughter. I reached out to the middle school yearbook staff to ask these questions, hoping for clarity.

2:21 p.m.

From HW

To: School

I wanted to touch base with potentially doing an honorary page for Aubreigh. That may already be in the works. I am not sure. If not, is there something we can do to dedicate a page to her?

2:23 p.m.

From: School

To: HW

Unfortunately, this has already been asked, and I was told that we would not be able to accommodate the request. I am sorry.

I stared at the screen in disbelief, the words blurring as hot tears welled in my eyes. It was nearly the end of the school day, and I didn't have it in me to type a response. My heart was pounding, my face flushed, and every part of me was screaming that this couldn't be real. Instead, as soon as the bell rang, I shot up from my desk, walked straight to my principal's office, and unraveled.

"This is why I'm so tired of this place!" I cried, the words tumbling out before I could even catch my breath. "I am over the attempts to erase my daughter."

She looked startled, confused. For once, she hadn't known what was going on, and she immediately ushered me into her office. I pulled out my phone, showed her the email, my hands shaking so hard I could barely hold it steady. She read it, her face tightening, and without hesitation, she reached for the phone to start making calls, trying to get me answers.

But there wasn't much that could happen in that moment. Bureaucracy doesn't move at the speed of a grieving mother's heart. And I had children waiting for me at home. So I left, my body trembling as I walked to my car, the ache in my chest making it hard to breathe.

As I drove away from the school, I knew. Something in me broke, and I couldn't unsee it, couldn't unfeel it. I knew I had to make a big change in my life. I wasn't just hurting.

The school's refusal to recognize my daughter, their willingness to brush her aside as if she never lived, was the final straw.

Since she had passed, so many small moments arose, ideas like putting up a banner for Aubreigh, wearing a pin, or honoring her in any way, things that might have offered me even the tiniest sliver of peace, they were crushed before they could breathe. It felt as though no one cared. The school district seemed more determined to stay quiet, to sweep everything under the rug, to cover their mistakes, than to acknowledge the life of a student they had failed or the grief of a teacher still standing in their classrooms.

To be shoved aside was painful enough, but to watch them behave as though my daughter never existed... that was unbearable. Others got to carry on, to celebrate their children in that school, while mine was erased. I felt disrespected, discarded, treated like nothing more than a number on a payroll, while Aubreigh was reduced to a test score in their system.

They had forgotten we were people... humans with hearts shattered by loss. And each day I walked those halls, reminded of the empty space where my daughter should have been, the weight of it all became utterly unbearable.

The workplace had become toxic, not by design, but through subtle, soul-crushing constraints. Requests to keep silent about Aubreigh. Office gossip wrapped in shushing tones. Colleagues and administration were watching my social media. Micromanagement that went beyond professionalism into an invasion of grief. It was like I was expected to put my heart away while working for the school district. Layers of emotional labor built up, as I pretended to be "fine."

By January 8th, I knew I couldn't keep showing up every day in a place that expected me to be silent about my own child, to set aside my grief and pretend that I was whole when I was anything but. I tried. I truly did. That first week after Christmas break, I gave it everything I had.

I had given everything I had to that place for nine years, but even more importantly, after losing Aubreigh, I had given everything I had to those children, to those walls. But that first week after Christmas break, it became clear that no matter how hard I tried, my efforts would never be enough. I needed to be grieving. I needed to be healing. So I told myself the truth: this wasn't failure. This was survival.

I was teaching, advancing in my grad program to obtain my master's degree, grieving the intestine-crushing loss of my child, helping my children grieve, and doing everything I could to appear stable, all while drowning. It was clear: I needed to step away not just for a day, but for healing.

That week, I sat with my therapist, then my doctor. Each one of them, in their own way, told me the same thing: *you cannot carry all of this at once.* My therapist reminded me that grief is not something that can be scheduled between lesson plans and faculty meetings. She said, "Heather, your nervous system is in overdrive. You're not just tired, you're depleted. And the environment you're in is re-traumatizing you every single day." She explained that what I was experiencing was compounded trauma, layered stress, and symptoms of PTSD. Sleep disruption, panic, exhaustion, intrusive thoughts. All signals that my brain was in survival mode, not a place to teach and nurture children. She was kind but firm: "If you keep pushing through this, you risk a full collapse. Your body and mind are telling you to stop."

My doctor, looking at me not just as a patient but as a mother, a friend, nodded and said, "Heather, it is not a weakness to step away. It is not a weakness to need medicine, to need time. This is what FMLA is for. You need time to heal, time for therapy, time for your family, time to breathe."

They all agreed: this was not optional. It was necessary.

So on January 8th, 2024, I walked into my boss, the principal's office, and told her what I had decided. My voice was steady, but my hands trembled. "I need to go back out on leave," I said. "My doctor and therapist agree this is the best choice for me right now."

The conversation was difficult because how do you explain to someone who hasn't lived it that walking into your workplace feels like walking into a battlefield? That every bulletin board, every classroom, every hallway is a ghost? That your chest tightens when you pass the playground, knowing your child once laughed there, but never will again?

I told her that my last day would be Friday, January 12th. That I didn't know when or even if I'd be ready to come back that school year. It might be halfway through, it might be a full year. I wasn't going to force a timeline on my healing.

She nodded, but I could see the tension in her face. Administrators often want certainty. They want dates, forms, and boxes checked. And I didn't have any of that to give. I had only honesty: *I cannot be here. Not right now.*

Going out on FMLA, the Family and Medical Leave Act, isn't as simple as just saying you need time. There are forms to fill out, signatures to gather, and documentation to provide.

My doctor and therapist both wrote formal notes recommending leave, citing the medical necessity of time away from work due to grief, trauma, and mental health. I submitted paperwork through the district office, officially requesting leave under FMLA protections. The policy allowed me up to twelve weeks of unpaid leave with job protection, though in education, every district interprets it slightly differently.

It was exhausting and ironic that the very act of trying to heal came with so much paperwork and justification. Forms asked me to describe the "condition" preventing me from working, as though grief for a child could be summed up in a sentence. But I filled them out anyway, attaching the notes, making the calls, doing everything the system required.

At the same time, I felt conflicted. Teachers are made to feel guilty for stepping away, even when it's life or death. Colleagues might whisper, administrators might worry about coverage. But I reminded myself, this district had not cared about me, my child, or the agony we'd been living in. They had tried to silence me, to push my grief into a corner, to make my pain less visible because it was inconvenient for their image. They had watched me crumble under the weight of loss and still expected me to keep up appearances. I was not abandoning anyone. I was taking the only step that could keep me whole.

That last week, I finished lesson plans for the substitute, prepared everything for the students through May, five full months of work, laid out week by week, through the end of the school year, just in case. I had everything organized by the weeks, by the subjects, homework, classwork, tests, everything to make it easy for whoever would be stepping into my place. My students deserved consistency, not another upheaval. They and their families had already been precious, kind, and patient with me during the hardest months of my life, giving me grace when I needed it most. The last thing I wanted was for my grief, or the way the district had treated me, to ripple out and hurt them. I cleaned my desk and tried to prepare my students for my absence without giving them details too heavy for children to carry. Inside, I was torn. Teaching had been my calling. But the truth was undeniable: I wasn't walking away from my students, I was walking toward my healing.

On Friday, January 12th, 2024, I closed my classroom door for what would be the last time in that season of my life. I didn't know when I would return. I only knew I couldn't stay.

Walking away from the classroom felt like closing one chapter without knowing if I'd ever step back into it again. But even as that door shut behind me, another was opening. In the quiet that followed, without the daily chaos of lesson plans and hallways, I suddenly had space, space to feel the grief fully, but also space to listen. And what I kept hearing, over and over, was the pull toward something greater. If I couldn't be in the classroom teaching, then maybe God was calling me to a different kind of work, a mission that extended beyond four walls. That still, small voice inside of me kept whispering that Aubreigh's story wasn't meant to end in silence.

Over and over again, it felt like God was placing signs in my path. Gentle nudges. Urgent reminders. Proof that this mission wasn't optional. That somehow, through all this pain, we were being called to turn tragedy into purpose. The moments came too often and too perfectly timed to be dismissed as a coincidence.

By January, I allowed myself to slowly reenter the world of social media, but cautiously, one app at a time. I couldn't afford to overwhelm myself. And yet, no matter which screen I opened, whether it was the news, a message, or a scroll through a feed, there it was again: another story, another cry for help, another parent mourning a child. Teens were still struggling. Parents were still searching for answers. Families like mine were still breaking under the weight of grief.

And somehow, in the middle of my own devastation, I saw that my words mattered. The raw posts, the unfiltered truth, the moments when I spoke honestly about loss. They weren't just pouring out into the void. They were landing on hearts that needed them. They were making a difference.

I received message after message.

A teenager would write: *"This saved my life."*

Another whispered, *"I thought I was alone. I'm not,"* and *"Because of your story, I told my mom what I was going through."*

Parents reached out, sometimes with trembling gratitude, saying: *"Thank you. Because of you, we're finally talking to our kids."*

"You made us realize we needed to check in with our daughter. We're talking now because of you."

These weren't just words on a screen; they were confirmations. They were proof that the pain I carried could be turned into purpose.

Even small encounters in day-to-day life became confirmations. A mom stopped me in a store to say she and her son prayed for us every night. Teens messaged me quietly, grateful just to be seen. Each interaction felt like God whispering: *keep going*. Small encounters, big reminders. Over and over again, it became clear that this wasn't just about surviving my grief. It was about using it. It was about fighting for kids like Aubreigh, kids who deserved hope, safety, and a future.

I could see that my willingness to share our story was making a difference. I couldn't save Aubreigh, but maybe just maybe I could help save another child. I could help another family never have to deal with this unbearable pain.

It was then that I knew the idea of The Aubreigh Wyatt Foundation couldn't wait. This wasn't a "someday" thing. It was now. That tiny spark had first lit back in September, in the rawest days after losing Aubreigh, when I sat in a psychiatrist's office and a parent turned to me for guidance. Even in my own wreckage, I felt the nudge—*this is bigger than me, this is needed*. At the time, it was just a whisper, a fragile thought I tucked away. But by January, with every story I read, every message I received, and every sign God placed in my path, that whisper grew louder. I couldn't ignore it anymore. What had begun as a flicker of an idea in the aftermath of unthinkable loss had become a mission I could no longer put off.

Building the Vision

From the beginning, I wanted the foundation to be everything, to cover every need, every resource, every kind of help. I imagined therapy centers, healing retreats, safe spaces for teens to rediscover themselves. But the reality set in quickly: I couldn't do it all at once. If I wanted this foundation to live, I had to start with focus.

So I narrowed the mission down to three core goals:

1. **Resources:** I wanted the foundation to be a hub, a place where parents and children could find links, talking points,

therapists, counselors, and immediate guidance. No one should ever feel like they don't know where to turn.

2. **Financial Assistance:** I knew too many families faced the unthinkable choice: counseling or groceries, therapy or bills. A child's healing should never hinge on a dollar amount. The foundation would provide grants and assistance to cover therapy and counseling when families couldn't.

3. **Access to Care:** Especially in Mississippi, the shortage of therapists and counselors was staggering. Waiting lists stretched six months long. Children in crisis can't wait six months. They can't wait six weeks. I wanted the foundation to fill that gap, to connect, to advocate, and eventually, to expand the pool of qualified professionals.

Those were the immediate priorities. But in the back of my heart, there was a bigger vision, a long-term dream of building a true rehabilitation and healing center. A place where kids could stay, work intensively with experts, and take the time they needed to heal. I knew that was the five-year plan, but the seeds were planted from the very beginning.

So two days after my pause on teaching, on January 14th, 2024, I filed the paperwork to officially establish The Aubreigh Wyatt Foundation. It was almost poetic, really. One chapter pausing, possibly closing, another beginning. That date is etched into my memory: the day The Aubreigh Wyatt Foundation officially applied to be recognized both in the state of Mississippi and as a federal nonprofit.

Getting a nonprofit off the ground isn't simple. It's a process that requires structure, signatures, and patience. I was new at all of this. I was going in blind with no clue as to what I was doing. The process was overwhelming. It wasn't just a matter of signing a paper. We had to name the foundation. That seemed like the easy part, but no. We had to make sure the name *The Aubreigh Wyatt Foundation* was legally available in Mississippi and not already taken. It would define everything, from our legal identity to our website. Every nonprofit in Mississippi must have a registered agent, a person with an in-state address to accept official mail and legal notices. We filed the articles of incorporation with the Secretary of State, declaring our mission and purpose: charitable, educational, and faith-driven. We created the initial Board of Directors.

So I carefully chose people for the initial Board of Directors who shared the vision and could guide decisions with wisdom: a treasurer, a secretary, and supporting directors who believed in the mission.

Then came the bylaws; these documents became our playbook, spelling out officer roles, meeting rules, and protections against personal gain. We applied for a federal Employer Identification Number from the IRS, which was necessary for taxes and banking. With the Articles, bylaws, and EIN in hand, we opened a dedicated nonprofit account, keeping the Foundation's money separate, accountable, and transparent. We then filed the application for the 501(c) (3) IRS Form 1023, a detailed application that included our mission statement, board member list, bylaws, projected budgets, and planned activities. It was expensive and time-consuming, but it was the key to federal recognition and tax-deductible donations.

We learned quickly that nonprofits don't just start; they must maintain. Annual IRS Form 990s, annual reports to the state, board minutes, and renewal of registrations all became part of our ongoing responsibility. We had to find a CPA. There was so much more to this than I had anticipated, and I just wanted to help! But one step at a time, one more thing checked off, and the foundation was slowly coming to life. It was overwhelming, but it gave the Foundation its skeleton. The legal framework to carry the heart. Every step felt like another confirmation: this wasn't just an idea anymore, it was real. I knew it would take months, maybe even years, to get this going and off the ground, but we were starting!

The Foundation's identity needed a face. We wanted the foundation to have an identity, something instantly recognizable and deeply tied to Aubreigh. A daily reminder to me to keep going, and a way to honor Aubreigh. Her legacy was guiding us to save others. The image that spoke the loudest was an artwork created after her passing. At first glance, it's an image of Aubreigh walking away in her white dress. The picture had been edited to add angel wings at her back, a ribbon woven into the design, and birds flying free into the sky. But the details are what make it sacred.

The angel wings softly extend from her back, symbolizing both her Heavenly presence and the way she continues to watch over others. They remind us that although she is not physically here, her spirit guides, protects, and lifts others.

At the hem of the dress, there was a tiny four-leaf clover. A detail so small, yet so deeply significant. It symbolized her birthday, March 17th, St. Patrick's Day. That tiny clover was a reminder of the day God gave her to me, and the day she blessed the world with her light.

Woven into the logo is the suicide awareness ribbon. The ribbon carries pink blended with purple, keeping part of the traditional teal and purple awareness ribbon while infusing it with something uniquely Aubreigh. Pink was her favorite color, bright, joyful, and vibrant. Together, they feel hopeful, lighthearted, and free-spirited, just like her personality.

Pink runs throughout the design, not just because it's bright and beautiful but because it was *her* favorite color. Pink was her personality.

The birds aren't simply in the background. They rise from the ribbon itself. It shows that freedom and hope can still take flight even out of the weight of awareness, struggle, and remembrance. The birds symbolize release, transformation, and the spreading of love beyond one life. They remind us that while pain is real, it can give rise to something greater: awareness, healing, and the courage to keep going. Just as they soar upward from the ribbon, they carry the message that even in loss, love continues to rise and spread. A symbol of hope.

Back inside the ribbon, one of the most meaningful details of the Foundation's logo is something that might be overlooked at first glance: the semicolon placed inside the awareness ribbon. A semicolon. To many people, a semicolon is just punctuation. But in the mental health and suicide prevention community, it carries profound meaning. A semicolon represents a pause, not an end. In writing, an author uses a semicolon when they could have ended a sentence, but instead chose to continue. That symbolism has been adopted around the world as a reminder that life, too, can continue even after dark chapters. It stands for survival. It stands for strength. It says: *Your story isn't over.* For the Foundation's logo, the semicolon inside the ribbon became more than just a design choice; it became a declaration. It was a way of saying to every child, every parent, every struggling soul who sees it: *you still have more to write. Your life has more pages. This isn't the end of your story.* For me, as Aubreigh's mother, it is also deeply personal. I couldn't change the ending of her story, but I could fight to change the ending of someone else's. That semicolon, tucked inside the ribbon, is both a memorial and a mission. It honors what was lost, while fiercely protecting what can still be saved. Every time I look at the logo, the semicolon reminds me that although my daughter's life ended far too soon, I can choose to continue her story by pouring love, hope, and purpose into others. It symbolizes the continuation of hers, mine, and the countless children and families the Foundation will serve.

And then, the dress. It wasn't just a dress from a picture. It was *the* dress, the very same one she was buried in. The details are hard to even write, but they make the image sacred. It represents innocence, purity, and the journey forward, even when we cannot see what lies ahead. That dress carried her in life, and in death, and now it carries her forward in every shirt, every logo, every piece of the Foundation. Every feather in her wings, every curve in the ribbon, every line mattered. This wasn't just art. It was a memory. It was love.

That became the official logo of The Aubreigh Wyatt Foundation.

For me, it wasn't just a design. Every time I saw it on paper, on a shirt, on a website, it was like seeing Aubreigh again, a constant reminder of her presence. It symbolized healing, remembrance, and a mission bigger than my grief. It meant that while my daughter's footsteps had stopped here, her walk continued through the lives of others we could save.

With approvals and designs in hand, we turned to fundraising. The very first product we launched was simple: t-shirts.

We collaborated with a manufacturer, working through details most people never think about, such as shirt styles, fabrics, printing methods, and ink colors. We sent the logo files, checked proofs, and debated between colors until we found what felt right. We ordered prototypes, tested quality, and prepared the first run.

Our first fundraising effort was simple but powerful: shirts. We launched those two designs. The official Foundation shirt with the angel logo, and the *Live Like Aubreigh* pink shirt. The shirts were more than fabric. They were wearable awareness. They spread her name, her story, her mission. And they gave us our very first stream of funding.

Those weeks after stepping away from school were a strange mix of exhaustion and renewal. Without the daily drain of the classroom, I had time. Time to pray, read devotionals, attend therapy, and actually breathe. Time to grieve properly. Time to sit with my children and help them through their own storms.

And time to pour myself into myself, mourning, the foundation.

By the end of January, the Foundation was no longer just an idea or paperwork. It was alive.

But even as I tried to navigate my decision to step away from the classroom, the atmosphere at the school only made things harder. It was suffocating. What should have been a place of support and understanding turned into a place of silence and control.

I thought that leaving would bring relief. I believed that once I was no longer in the building every day, I would have space to heal. And in some ways, I did. I finally had the quiet to focus on therapy, my family, and the Foundation. But the toxicity of the district didn't end at the door.

Leaving should have given me peace. Instead, it clarified how far the school district was willing to go to erase me and, worse, to erase Aubreigh.

Friends of mine who I worked alongside for years texted me things like...

Hey, I'm sorry for not reaching out sooner.
We've been told to stay away and keep out of it.
Heather, I'm so sorry for not contacting you before now.
The admin has clarified that we are not to talk about Aubreigh.
We've been told not to contact you. I had to, though. I'm so sorry.

Knowing people wanted to reach out, comfort, and acknowledge the truth of what I was going through, but were afraid to, made me furious. The administration had made it clear: this was not something to be spoken about openly. My own daughter's life and memory were treated like a liability to the district. Instead of honoring her, they hushed her. Instead of compassion, they enforced silence.

I saw how fear spread through the staff. I learned from friends that they were pulled into offices, spoken to behind closed doors, and left shaken. The message was always the same: *don't say too much, don't get involved, don't step out of line.* It was an unspoken gag order, and people complied because they feared what would happen if they didn't. And so the silence grew.

But eventually, friends sent me snapshots of emails and text messages from the administration.

Emails showed just how far the administration would go to silence people. Teachers were pulled into offices, reminded of the "expectations." Conversations about me, Aubreigh, and anything uncomfortable were shut down before they began. Staff lived under a cloud of fear, fear of saying the wrong thing, fear of being associated with me, fear of acknowledging the truth.

Even though I wasn't there, I could feel it. The micromanagement. The monitoring. The way my social media was still being watched, dissected, as if grief could be managed with policies and spreadsheets. It was invasive, dehumanizing, and exhausting.

The friendships I thought were safe eventually cracked under the pressure. Those colleagues and friends who once comforted me, who once joked with me to ease the tension. The friends who shared messages about the absurdity of the situation, the micromanaging, and the way the administration, especially our Principal, overstepped boundaries and monitored everything I did. They all texted, sent videos, and recordings; they knew it was wrong. They said not to say anything, not to put their name in it, but they wanted me to know. Sarcasm was our coping mechanism, our only way to keep from screaming. "Your friend," my colleague would text, referring to our tyrant boss, the principal, with biting irony, as if to say: *Look at how they're treating you again.* These friends who knew it was wrong, who had loved not only me, but my children as well, eventually fell silent. Fear has a way of isolating people, of making even friends pull back.

By the end of February, so many friendships had faded, the threat of termination and reprimands too strong, another reminder of how isolating grief had become in a place that should have been my refuge. My friend. Another casualty of the district's obsession with control.

For me, that silence was louder than any words. It confirmed what I already knew: I could not return to that building. I could not exist in a place that punished compassion and feared truth. I could not go back to a workplace that treated my child like a problem to be hidden.

For weeks, the chaos with the school district consumed so much of my energy that it was hard to focus on anything else. But life didn't pause just because I was at war with silence and control. Even in grief, everyday life kept moving forward around me; my kids still had places to be, milestones to meet, and memories to make. And as January pressed on, those moments came whether I felt ready or not.

Late in January, Taylor went on a youth group trip to Tennessee. It was the same youth group Aubreigh had traveled with just months earlier in the summer. Watching Taylor pack her bag was like opening a wound, like being split in two. She was brave enough to step into something new, strong enough to go even when I knew her heart carried its own quiet ache. On the other hand, it tore me apart because I knew how much Aubreigh had loved that trip, how badly she would have wanted to go again, and how this was something the girls should have done together. I could picture them side by side, whispering on the bus, sharing snacks, probably fighting over snacks and clothes, actually.

There were tears, so many tears, but also pride. It was Taylor's first time going away without me since Aubreigh had passed away, and as hard as it was to let her go, I knew it was good for her. Grief carried both emotions at once: the ache of what was missing and the relief of what was still possible.

When Taylor came home from Tennessee, she was glowing. She

had gotten everything out of that trip, and I had prayed for her. Time to worship, to snowboard, to laugh with friends, to just be free for a little while from the heaviness of life and the chaos we'd all been living in. Seeing her smile, hearing her stories—it gave me a flicker of relief. For a moment, she had been able to breathe again, and that mattered.

But almost as soon as she returned, another milestone loomed, the middle school winter formal. And with it came another wave of bittersweet emotions, because at the last Winter Formal dance, Aubreigh was with us. The year before, she had sat at our dining room table, perfectly centered between two windows, because she insisted on having the best natural light. Makeup was scattered everywhere, foundation bottles tipped on their sides, mascara wands rolling toward the edge, eyeshadow palettes open like tiny paint trays. I curled her hair in soft spirals while she sat there grinning, and then I brushed her cheeks with blush, lined her eyes, swept mascara onto her lashes, and finished with her lips. She was all dolled up, glowing, and so excited to walk into that dance like it was her own little runway.

So here we were. Eighth grade, and her friends were preparing for this year's dance. I couldn't help but think about what should have been. Aubreigh begging to pick out dresses, wanting her nails done, getting dolled up with all the giggles of her friends. She would have been ecstatic.

So when this year's winter formal arrived, and I saw her friends preparing, laughing, and slipping on their dresses, it gutted me. I could picture her right there, begging me to help pick out shoes, chattering about which hairstyle she wanted, twirling in the mirror to make sure every detail was perfect, and rushing me to get her there on time!

She should have been there.

Instead, I stood on the sidelines, grieving. Kelly, Ryker's stepmom, who does photography on the side, took pictures of the group of eighth-graders who were in or acquainted with Aubreigh's group of friends as a favor to me. Organizing twenty-five to thirty middle schoolers is no easy task; there was the usual chaos of dresses being adjusted, jackets being straightened, kids giggling and wandering out of line. But eventually they lined up, one group after another, ready to be photographed.

First, the girls posed together, arms linked, faces glowing in the way only teenage girls can glow, their dresses catching the light as they leaned into each other. They laughed, adjusting curls, smoothing sequins, whispering little jokes meant only for them. Then the boys took their turn, standing shoulder to shoulder, trying so hard to look grown and serious, but their grins betrayed them, breaking into laughter they couldn't hold back. Finally, everyone crowded together for one big picture, twenty-five, maybe thirty kids—all dressed up, buzzing with energy, ready for a night of music, dancing, and memories they would never forget.

And right there in the middle, they held up a large canvas photo of Aubreigh.

The sight stole the breath from my chest. Her face, framed by her friends, lifted high as if she were still among them. My eyes blurred with tears as I took it in. It was beautiful and devastating all at once. She was there, and yet she wasn't. Seeing her in that photo surrounded by the kids she should have been standing beside was proof she hadn't been forgotten. But it was also a gut-punch reminder of all she was missing. I could almost see her, radiant, twirling in her dress, throwing her head back in laughter. Instead, she was two-dimensional, frozen in time, a photograph carried by friends who loved her enough to make sure her presence was felt, even if only as a symbol.

I stood there, holding myself together on the outside, but inside I was splitting open.

And then my eyes caught the other moms. They clustered along the sidelines, phones out, cameras clicking, their smiles wide and unguarded. They fussed with curls that had fallen loose, straightened ties, brushed invisible lint from shoulders. They looked so proud, so full of joy, capturing every detail of their babies on this milestone night. I watched them, and the sharpest pang of envy cut through me. Because I should have been there too, not just standing on the outside, but fussing over Aubreigh, smoothing her dress, fastening her heels, laughing as she rolled her eyes at me for taking too many pictures. I should have been the mom behind the camera, documenting her glow, her laughter, her joy.

But instead, I stood with empty hands. Empty arms. A hollow where my daughter should have been.

In that moment, I felt like I had been pushed into a cruel, invisible club that no mother wants to join. The "dead child mom" club. And I was the only member present. No one else there knew the weight of watching your child's peers pose for pictures while your own child existed only on canvas. No one else felt the sharp edge of envy slicing into love, or the suffocating loneliness of knowing life had moved forward for everyone else, while I was anchored to this gaping hole.

The loneliness pressed down on me until it was hard to breathe. My grief wasn't just sadness; it was layered with anger and despair, too. Anger at the unfairness, despair at the permanence, and an aching love that had nowhere to land.

She should have been there. God, she should have been there.

By the time the night ended, I was emotionally wrung out. Raw in a way that lingered for days. The winter formal had reminded me that grief doesn't just roar on anniversaries or holidays, it seeps into the ordinary milestones too. The ones where her absence screamed loudest. And just when I thought I might catch my breath, life pressed forward again, indifferent to whether I was ready.

As January slipped into February, I was still in survival mode. Every day felt like a balancing act between managing grief, caring for Taylor and Ryker, and simply forcing myself to keep moving. On February 6th, Ryker had his tonsils removed. Just a routine surgery, in and out. Both Taylor and Aubreigh had gone through it before, and rationally, I knew it wasn't anything major. But once you've buried a child, logic doesn't quiet the fear. My body betrayed me, spiraling straight into fight-or-flight. My stomach twisted until I was nauseous, nearly sick with panic, terrified that something might go wrong. That's what grief does: it rewires you. Everything feels like the next possible tragedy waiting to happen.

Meanwhile, the weight of my professional life pressed harder. I was on FMLA, and deep down I already knew I couldn't return to the district for the next school year. They had shown me their true color, silencing, scrutinizing, refusing to honor my daughter in even the smallest ways. I was unraveling under their pressure, and finally, I admitted to myself that going back wasn't just unwise; it was impossible.

But admitting that didn't bring relief. It brought guilt and fear. Teaching was all I had ever known. It wasn't just a job, it was my calling, my identity, my steady paycheck. It was the career I had fought so hard to reach, the one I had sacrificed sleep and sanity for, pushing through college as a single mom so I could build stability and give my kids the life I never had. Walking away felt unthinkable, almost like betraying something sacred. It was more than leaving a classroom; it was letting go of the very thing that had shaped so much of who I was, who my family was.

Still, the internal tug-of-war was relentless. One side screamed, *Don't let go of what you know.* The other whispered, *You can't keep killing yourself to keep everyone else afloat.* And hovering above all of it was the fear of the unknown.

And then, in the middle of that storm, God nudged me. My friend

Kassi had mentioned a position she thought I'd be a good fit for, that an opening had just been released. It was at a company she'd worked for before, and she had nothing but good things to say about it. She told me maybe I could start fresh there, maybe at the end of the school year, maybe sooner. At first, I brushed it off. Teaching was all I had ever known. But the more I thought about it, the more it felt like God whispering: *You're done here. It's time for something new.*

I told her I was still on FMLA, that I wasn't sure I could handle even interviewing for something even knowing that I wouldn't go to work for them for several months, but she reassured me again and again. Reminding me that with this company, the process could take a while—background checks, orientation, paperwork. "Just get the application in," she urged. "Even if you're not ready now, by the time it's all said and done, you may be."

One evening, between helping Ryker rest and trying to keep my own head above water, I finally sat down and filled out the application. Honestly, I didn't expect anything to come of it. My days were still consumed with grief, therapy, raising two kids, and building the foundation. I could barely imagine what "something different" might even look like. At that point, I was still officially on FMLA. February had just begun, and my plan was straightforward: take the time I was medically allowed, do the hard work of healing, and then either return to finish out the school year with my students in the spring or extend my leave for the remainder of the school year if I wasn't ready.

Submitting the application wasn't me abandoning teaching or trying to slip quietly into something else. It was simply me acknowledging that this process—if it went anywhere at all—would take months. The application felt less like a career move and more like handing it to God: *What will be, will be. If this is a door You want opened, open it. If not, keep it closed.*

I knew from the start that nothing about it would be quick. There would be background checks, orientations, and all the red tape that could stretch for weeks, even months. In my mind, this was never about walking away mid-stride. It was about being ready if, and only if, God aligned it that way.

I had already told myself that if the company did call back with an offer, I would be upfront. I'd explain that I was still under contract as a teacher, on medical leave, and couldn't start until after the school year ended. For now, I could go through the process, prepare, and see if this seed grew into something. Submitting that application was simply me making space for the possibility that healing might lead me somewhere new.

In my mind, it was nothing more than planting a tiny seed of possibility. Maybe it would grow into something new, maybe it wouldn't. But hitting "submit" gave me a flicker of hope in a season when hope was so hard to come by.

Several days later, when the email came through offering me a position, I hesitated. Part of me wondered if I was ready for something new, if I could handle change when everything in my life already felt so unstable. But another part of me knew: I had nothing to lose. If nothing else, it was a step, a chance to see if there was life outside the battlefield I had been trudging through for months.

Walking into that interview, I carried all of my uncertainty with me, but something surprising happened. The conversation flowed. The questions felt natural. For the first time in a long time, I didn't feel scrutinized or silenced. I felt like myself, capable, confident, alive. When it ended, I walked out with a strange flicker of hope I hadn't felt in months. And a few days later, when they called back with an offer, I couldn't help but wonder if this was God's way of confirming what I had been too scared to say out loud: *That chapter is closed. It's time for something new.*

The process, of course, wasn't immediate. There were background

checks, drug tests, physicals, hearing exams, and orientation require-
ments. They reassured me that it would take time to get everything
lined up anyway, and since I was still on FMLA, I told myself I could
see it through without pressure. It was almost a relief to think about
something new, something that wasn't colored by grief and control.

But then came the part that left me reeling. Somehow, word got
back to the district. While I was still in the quiet, behind-the-scenes
stage, background checks, health exams, orientation paperwork, not
even hired anywhere else yet, just preparing myself for a possible
opportunity, my phone lit up with a text from my principal: *"Are you
planning to take another job?"*

The timing was too exact, too uncanny, too precise to be coincidence. My heart dropped. It wasn't that I was hiding anything. I'd
been transparent and respectful. But how did she know? How had
a private application, a step toward my future after the school year,
already made it into the district's hands?

It wasn't just unnerving; it was invasive. And in that moment,
something in me shifted. This wasn't the first time my professional
boundaries had been crossed. For months. I'd felt the slow creep of
control. Emails monitored. Questions about my off-duty life. Subtle
reminders that my loyalty was being watched. A job that should have
been a safe place to work, then go home and breathe, had become a
place where every move felt scrutinized, where privacy was not just
ignored but quietly stripped away.

This text was the tipping point. After everything, the exhaustion,
the overreach, the constant sense of being observed. I realized I wasn't
imagining it. They *were* monitoring my life. Even the smallest steps I
took to plan for my future were being reported back before I'd even
had a chance to act on them. And that realization ignited a mix of
anger, grief, and resolve so strong it left me shaking.

On February 12th, my hands trembling but my words steady, I

sat down and wrote to the superintendent. This wasn't an impulsive act. It was the culmination of months of pressure, a boundary finally drawn, my way of saying *not again*.

To: ██████████████████████

From: ████████████████████████

Good Afternoon,

I am compelled to address recent distressing occurrences that have deeply troubled me. Firstly, I must express my profound dismay at the recent unethical conduct that has transpired.

Currently, I am on FMLA leave from my position at the school due to significant anxiety, PTSD, and insomnia, primarily stemming from issues within the district. I also want to reiterate that my FMLA only stipulates that I am unable to fulfill the responsibilities of my current position at the school.

Regrettably, my privacy was egregiously breached when discussions regarding my FMLA were held in a public setting within the school's office. Furthermore, I find it deeply concerning that both ████████ and █████████████, administrators of my school, sought to inquire about my employment status with the assumption that I was working elsewhere.

██████████ and █████████████ attempted to reach out to individuals asking if I was employed at another place.

My third complaint is that they also called the said business and asked the HR department if I was an employee with them. Upon several phone calls from other individuals to me, and screenshots I was able to verify with certainty, they were reaching out to others asking about me, disclosing my information, and violating my privacy.

From around November 2023 to the present, I have been harassed, questioned, and reprimanded for things because of the district's dissatisfaction with my approach to bringing awareness to the death of my daughter. Despite being on FMLA, the harassment persists, exacerbating my trauma and compounding existing anxiety and PTSD.

I implore immediate action to rectify these egregious breaches of privacy and unethical behavior within the district.

In light of these circumstances, I wish to tender my resignation from my role as a teacher within the ██████ ██████████ School District. Additionally, I want to clarify that I will not be seeking contract renewal for the forthcoming school year.

Best,
Heather Wyatt

I pressed send, my stomach in knots. I had officially resigned. I should have felt relief. But instead, within minutes, the chaos began.

The moment I sent in my resignation, the district showed its true colors in a way I'll never forget. Instead of handling things professionally, they scrambled into damage control and intimidation mode.

The Texts Begin

1:03 p.m. A message popped up from a colleague:

> ███ just asked me if I heard anything about you working somewhere else? I said no and looked shocked. She said someone called her over the weekend. I told her we text here and there but I haven't heard anything. She said she'd have to check into that. Then she says maybe you're just trying it out.

I stared at the screen in disbelief. "Trying it out?" My entire life was unraveling, and they were treating it like gossip to pass around an office.

I texted back, furious:

> I wonder who said something because no one knows I even had an interview!!

But it didn't stop.

Another message came, this time from Nick.

"A friend of mine just called me," he said. *"He works security at that company you applied to. The school district's resource officers, not even HR, not administrators, the SROs have been calling him, asking if you're working there."*

My stomach turned. They weren't just quietly questioning staff anymore; they were reaching into my personal life, using law-enforcement contacts to pry. School resource officers, people whose job is supposed to be keeping students safe, were calling a company's

security office to try to track me down. It wasn't even in their job description. And now Nick's friend, through no fault of his own, was pulled into the middle of it. I felt sick. They weren't just questioning staff anymore. They were dragging my personal relationships into this.

That was the moment it hit me: they were willing to go beyond the walls of the school, beyond their roles, to monitor me. My private plans weren't private at all.

My colleague kept trying to reassure me:.

But minutes later:

 She just called me in.

I typed fast, desperate:

What did she say?

The reply hit hard:

She told me about the email. Someone from the office said she was asking about it.

The Witch Hunt

The texts went back and forth. My colleague confessed our principal had cornered her.

I could feel her fear through the screen. Our principal wanted a target, and she had decided to make it me, and anyone who dared stand by me.

150

I reassured her again:

> Don't let her bully you. She just wants a target. Instead of emailing me back, she runs to you.

By now, my phone was buzzing nonstop. Other friends warned me that our Principal was spreading rumors through the office. My hands shook as I typed, adrenaline pumping, feeling both paranoid and justified. I wasn't imagining things; this was happening in real time.

And then, out of nowhere, verification codes started flooding my phone.

The Lockout

> G-798352 is your Google verification code.

> G-486535 is your Google verification code.

> G-925496 is your Google verification code.

One after another, back-to-back.
Then the screen changed.
Your password was changed less than an hour ago.
I snapped a screenshot and sent it to my colleague:

> They're trying to log into my school email. Like, how the hell! Call me when you can.

Within minutes of my resignation, they were already trying to kick me out, change my access, erase me. I remember staring at my phone, sick to my stomach, thinking, *How is this happening? Why are they this desperate to erase me?*

And still, the gossip machine kept spinning. They acted like I was some kind of fugitive, like my healing and moving on was a crime they needed to investigate. My personal life was being dragged through the mud by the very people who should have respected my privacy and my grief.

This was the true face of the district: not compassion, not support, but intimidation, control, and harassment. They wanted me silenced, erased. And in their panic to control the story, they only proved what I had known all along: I was never safe in their hands.

Almost immediately, I began hearing from colleagues that the Principal was pulling other people into her office, pressing them for information, demanding to know what I was doing, who I had spoken to, and whether I was really going to work elsewhere. People texted me in a panic, saying she was "looking right at them" during questioning, insisting she wanted a target. It was like a witch hunt. Teachers were terrified, while at the same time, the principal stirred up paranoia and suspicion among them.

People were nervous, caught in the crossfire. They wanted to support me, but the fear of retaliation from the district was real.

The truth was undeniable: they didn't care about me, my grief, or my healing. They didn't care about Aubreigh. What they cared about was their reputation and control. About silencing me. About making sure no one saw the ugly truth of how they treated a grieving mother who dared to keep speaking out.

I had already been micromanaged, monitored, silenced, and reprimanded for honoring my daughter. I had endured their coldness and their attempts to erase her memory. But this? The gossiping, the HR calls, the password resets, the intimidation of staff, the outreach to my personal friends, it was beyond unprofessional. It was harassment. It was invasive. It was cruel.

In that moment, any lingering guilt I had about resigning was gone. I knew I had made the right choice because no one deserves to be treated this way, least of all a mother clawing her way through grief.

9

New Job

At first, I hadn't planned to start right away. My intention had been to finish out the school year before making the transition. But after resigning, after officially severing ties with the district, everything shifted. I was no longer under contract, no longer tethered to that system. A few weeks later, when the company finished the background checks, orientations, and screenings and called with an official offer, I surprised myself by saying yes. I decided to go ahead and take the position rather than wait.

When I stepped into my new role, it felt like entering an entirely different world. I walked through it with a mixture of excitement and nerves. For so long, I had been defined by the rhythm of school first as a college student, and then as a teacher. That environment demanded constant alertness: always being "on," always responsible for a room full of children. Even the smallest things, like taking a bathroom break or having a quiet lunch, were luxuries that didn't exist in that world. So, when I transitioned into a new career, this new corporate setting was a major adjustment.

After spending ten years in one environment, stepping into a new building where I didn't know a single person, where I didn't know where anything was, came with its own weight. I had to start over from scratch in so many ways, building connections, learning names, carving out my place. But there was also so much joy in it. I loved the learning curve, the newness of each day, the chance to stretch myself in ways I hadn't before. The adjustment was both startling and refreshing. Suddenly, I had moments of stillness. I could breathe. I could think. And I could be Heather, not just "Mrs. Wyatt," in charge of a classroom.

Teaching will always hold a special place in my heart. It was one of the greatest joys of my life, being in the classroom, connecting with students, and watching lightbulbs go off when something finally clicked. I loved the laughter, the creativity, the everyday moments of growth that happened in that space. But as much as I loved teaching, stepping into something new gave me the chance to see myself in a different light.

My new role was both intimidating and exhilarating at the same time. Instead of classrooms filled with children, I now sat in an administrative building surrounded by adults. People my age, people with similar experiences. It felt like I had finally stepped into a space where my education, skills, and talents had room to grow in new directions. I wasn't just managing lesson plans or grading papers anymore; I was using my computer skills, problem-solving, and analytical mind to contribute in ways I hadn't imagined before.

The first week was all about observing, learning, and taking it all in. Then, piece by piece, I was trusted to do the work myself, reviewing contracts, handling spreadsheets, analyzing purchase orders, and helping ensure everything lined up in the procurement process. It was challenging, but I loved it.

I had never envisioned myself working in a cubicle, yet I loved it. It felt like a little space that was mine, a place where I could focus and grow. Even the simple things, dressing up for work, carrying my coffee in, and sitting down at my desk, felt refreshing. As the weeks passed, I grew more confident. I became quicker with the tasks, more comfortable with the flow of the work, and gradually took on more.

Eventually, I was able to work on a schedule of two weeks in the office and two weeks remote, and that flexibility was a gift. Having the option to be home allowed me more time with my children and more balance in my days. It also gave me something I hadn't realized I was missing: the ability to truly disconnect when the workday ended. With teaching, my mind was always on; planning, worrying, grading, thinking about the next day. In this role, I could leave work at work. That difference felt like weight lifting from my shoulders, and in this chaotic time of my life, I truly needed that.

Teaching was never something I disliked; in fact, I loved it dearly. But in that season of life, stepping into something new was exactly what my soul needed. It gave me breathing room, a chance to reset, and a reminder that even in the midst of chaos, there can be peace and joy. I needed that, and I embraced it wholeheartedly.

Still, starting a nonprofit came with its own kind of learning curve. The advice I received early on was clear: build a financial cushion, let the funds sit, and establish stability before giving. But my mama heart couldn't do that. The need was already right in front of me. Families reaching out, children in crisis.

So instead of holding back, we opened the door. The very first profits from those shirts went directly toward paying for a child's therapy. Within weeks, another child was funded. It wasn't polished, it wasn't perfectly structured, and maybe it wasn't the "smart" financial strategy. But it was the right one. God had entrusted us with this mission.

And so, in those first months of 2024, the Foundation took its first shaky, sacred steps. With paperwork filed, shirts sold, and the first children receiving therapy through grants, the vision became reality. The work was messy, overwhelming, and emotional. But it was real. And it was only the beginning.

And then March came. Her birthday month. And with it, a weight pressing against my chest. The month had always been a countdown to joy, to cake and candles and presents wrapped in pink. But this time, it carried with it the heaviness of absence. The closer we drew to her birthday, the more the air seemed to shift. Every day brought waves of dread and longing, waves I couldn't stop, only brace myself against.

Even in the ordinary, the grief found its way in. When Taylor prepared for her prom—prom seemed to come early that year—the house should have been filled with two sisters laughing and rushing back and forth between bedrooms, clothes tossed on the bed, curling irons left plugged in, the air clouded with perfume. Instead, it was quiet. Taylor looked stunning in her gown, radiant in a way that caught me off guard, but there was a shadow in her eyes. She missed her sister. She smiled for pictures, but it was the kind of smile you give when part of your heart is elsewhere. Prom became one more reminder that we were learning to live with a hole in our family. Learning to make new memories without Aubreigh.

By the middle of March, the weight grew unbearable. For many years, I had celebrated my baby with gifts, laughter, and plans made just for her. Now I couldn't buy her anything, couldn't wrap a gift or hear her squeal when she opened it. So I chose something different, something that would stand tall and loud in a world that sometimes went on as if she had never existed. On March 14th, her billboard went up.

It was massive, stretching across the sky for everyone to see. Pink, her color, beamed across the background. The words read: *Happy Heavenly Birthday, Aubreigh. Deeply Missed, Forever Loved.* Along the bottom were four-leaf clovers, a nod to the fact that her birthday fell on St. Patrick's Day. The clovers connected her memory to the holiday itself, weaving her life into a day already marked by celebration. And at the left, her photograph, her in that white dress, so full of light and grace it almost hurt to look at. It stayed there the whole month of March, watching over the roads, watching over us. People pulled over to take pictures, some even standing beneath it with tears in their eyes. It was my gift to her, a way to shout into the silence: *She is still here. She still matters. She is still loved.*

Two days later, on March 16th, we decorated her gravesite. We brought armfuls of pink and white flowers, piling them high until her resting place looked like it had been draped in spring itself. Along with the fresh blooms, we also brought back two of the floral standing sprays that had stood at her funeral months before, one shaped like a cross, the other a four-leaf clover. We had saved them all this time, because they felt like too much of her to ever let go. For her birthday, I decorated them again, carefully weaving pink, white, and green flowers into their frames. The cross stood for her faith, and the clover, fitting for her St. Patrick's Day birthday. The air was cool, the kind of breeze that carried both comfort and ache. I knelt there, arranging petals, whispering words only she could hear. There was a tenderness in those moments, a fragile attempt at mothering her still, even in death.

The next day was Aubreigh's birthday, March 17th. The day the world first gave me my baby girl. That morning, the grief hit like a tidal wave. I remembered everything about the day she was born: the hospital lights, the sound of her first cry, the miracle of holding her tiny body against mine. How could it be that the same date, all these years later, held so much sorrow?

158

The morning of March 17th began with a tradition I had carried on since my children were little. Every year, no matter how busy we were or how early the day started, I always made pancakes for their birthdays. Taylor's day, Ryker's day, Aubreigh's day. It always began with pancakes at the table. We weren't big breakfast eaters otherwise, but birthdays were different. Birthdays deserved sweetness, warmth, and the smell of something special cooking on the griddle.

That morning, though, I hesitated. I wasn't sure if I could do it or if I had the strength to pour batter and flip pancakes, knowing she wouldn't be sitting down to eat them. But I also couldn't bear the thought of breaking the tradition. It felt like one more loss piled onto too many already. So I got up early, pulled out the mix, and made them anyway. The sound of the batter sizzling in the pan, the smell of butter browning it, was all achingly familiar.

When the pancakes were ready, I plated them like always. But this time, when we sat at the table, her chair wasn't empty. I placed a plate of pancakes where she always sat, the chair marked with a happy birthday ribbon tied around the back. Our family has this unspoken rhythm at the table. We always sat in the same places, without ever talking about it. So when I set her plate down in front of her spot, it felt natural, as if muscle memory had taken over.

We ate slowly, quietly. The pancakes were warm, golden, stacked high, but the air around the table was heavy with grief. Every bite carried both love and longing, the sweetness of tradition mixed with the bitterness of her absence. It was somber, difficult, and yet somehow sacred. A bittersweet way of beginning her day, keeping her place at the table, keeping her woven into the fabric of our family.

By lunchtime, it was time to make our way to the cemetery. It wasn't just me carrying this weight; it was all of us. Taylor, Ryker, and Nick were in the car with me. Together, we drove in silence under the gray. The sky was gray and overcast, which made the whole world feel muted. A light drizzle tapped against the windshield as we drove, and I remember feeling my stomach twitching from grief and worry. We had planned a beach celebration for later that evening, a gathering that meant so much to me, and I was terrified it would be washed out by rain. The clouds hung low, heavy with the threat of storms, as if the Heavens mourned with us.

At the gravesite, more family was waiting. My brother Jeff was there with his wife and their children, my nieces and nephews, Aubreigh's cousins, who had grown up alongside her. The sight of them all together with my children, the cousins, standing with us on this day, was both comforting and crushing. It reminded me that Aubreigh was not only my daughter and a sister, but a cousin, a niece, a friend, someone whose absence rippled outward through every branch of our family.

We gathered there in the damp air, pink and white flowers already covering her grave from the day before. The children stood close to one another, their small faces unsure how to carry the weight of the day, while the adults held tightly to one another, sharing silent looks of grief.

We stayed there together, letting the moments unfold gently. Memories of Aubreigh rose up and spilled into the air, not in polished speeches but in fragments, the kind of stories only family could tell. Someone remembered birthdays with balloons and pancakes, and another laughed through tears about her silly jokes in the car. We spoke of the way she doted on her little brother, the playful teasing she reserved for her sister, the way she could pull joy out of even the smallest moment.

Our words wove together with prayers, voices shaking as we asked God to hold her close, to let her feel the weight of our love even now. Between the memories and the prayers, there were silences too, the kind heavy with both mourning and remembrance. Sometimes, we

160

just sat with her, letting the quiet speak where words failed. Tears fell freely, but so did soft laughter, the bittersweet sound of remembering who she was and how much she had filled our lives.

Then came the small act that carried enormous weight. I bent down to the earth, to the candles pressed into the dirt months earlier: the "1" and the "3," marking her age. I pulled them up with trembling hands, replacing them with a "1" and a "4." She had not lived to see her fourteenth birthday here, but perhaps she had turned fourteen in Heaven. It was my way of honoring what should have been, my silent gift to her on this day.

After lingering there, after words, tears, and prayers had been spent, we knew it was time to carry on another tradition. For as long as I could remember, Aubreigh's birthday dinner had always meant hibachi. She loved the show of it all, the clang of metal on the grill, the fire bursting into the air, the onion volcano steaming tall. She always ordered medium-rare steak and generously poured yum-yum sauce over her rice. So we went again, all of us, trying to honor her by living that tradition.

I glanced at the empty spot where she should have been, imagining her rolling her eyes and giggling at the onion volcano, clapping when the chef tossed shrimp across the grill. The rice tasted the same, and the yum-yum sauce was just as sweet, but without her there, it was all different. Every bite was an act of remembrance.

When lunch was over, the day stretched forward, heavy and long. The rain had let up some, though clouds still lingered in the sky. For most of the afternoon, I kept glancing at the sky, half-praying, half-worrying. The clouds still hung low after our time at the gravesite, and I couldn't stop thinking about the beach celebration we had planned for the evening. It meant so much to me, to all of us, and the thought of it being ruined by rain felt unbearable.

And then, almost as if Heaven itself had heard, the skies began to clear. About forty-five minutes before everyone was set to arrive, the gray lifted. The drizzle stopped. The air softened. Puddles still glistened on the ground, and the sand was damp beneath our feet, but the storm had passed. The timing was so perfect it felt like a gift.

The sight before me stole my breath when we stepped onto the beach. Friends, family, classmates, neighbors, they came in waves, gathering one after another until the shoreline was alive with people. And everywhere I looked, there was pink. Shirts, ribbons, and clover pins, all shades of pink, swirled together, with green clovers mixed in for her St. Patrick's Day birthday. Pink balloons, green balloons, and butterfly balloons swayed in the wind, tethered to tables lined with cakes and cupcakes. One cake held a large "A" in frosting, symbolizing the girl we were there to honor.

It was like a sea of love rising up out of the wet sand. It was beautiful. It was heartbreaking. It was everything she deserved and everything we wished we didn't have to do this way. It felt like an army of love standing on the sand.

The salty air wrapped around us, mingling with the faint sweetness of cake. The sun sank lower and lower, painting the sky in shades of orange, pink, and gold until it looked like Heaven itself had spilled across the horizon. Waves lapped at the shore in a steady rhythm, like the heartbeat of the evening.

At one point, a single butterfly balloon broke free from the rest. I froze as I watched it drift upward, slowly, almost deliberately, against the colors of the sunset. It climbed higher and higher, until it was just a dot in the sky, and still I couldn't look away. It felt like her, like a piece of her spirit had taken flight right there in front of us. I stood there, staring, letting it carry a piece of my grief with it into the Heavens.

As the sun dipped below the horizon, we began passing candles down the line. One by one, each person took theirs, cupping it in their hands against the ocean breeze. Soon, the shoreline was dotted with small circles of light, each tiny flame flickering into the growing darkness. It wasn't just one candle on a cake; it was a vigil, a sea of people holding fire in their hands, tons of little lights glowing together.

When every candle was lit, we began to sing "Happy Birthday." The sound wavered and broke with tears, but it carried, soft and trembling, across the waves, as if the ocean itself was leaning in to listen. Through tears, the sound breaking and trembling, but strong enough to carry across the beach. The candles glowed, casting light on tear-streaked faces, until the song's final note. Together, we blew them out, sending the smoke upward like prayers, like love carried on the wind.

As the last candles flickered out and people began to gather their things, the celebration slowly unraveled into goodbyes. One by one, people drifted off, until all that was left was the sound of waves swallowing the shoreline and the rustle of balloons being packed away. There were long and tight hugs and moments of laughter at the memories that refused to fade. Some tears seemed endless, especially as I looked around and saw her friends laughing, singing, living, and knew she should have been standing among them. She should have been there, smiling widely, making TikToks on the sand, rolling her eyes at her mom being sentimental.

I remember loading the car, piece by piece, folding tables, empty cake pans, tangled strings of balloons. My body moved, but my heart felt numb. Surrounded by family and friends who loved her, who loved us, I should have felt comfort. And in some ways, I did. Yet beneath it all was a gnawing emptiness, an ache that no amount of company could fill. The celebration ended, but the ache did not.

The house's stillness pressed down like a weight when I crawled into bed that night. Her friends' laughter, the music, the sight of that butterfly balloon drifting into the sunset, they all replayed in my mind like a cruel reminder of what had been lost. And when the quiet finally settled, when there was nothing left to distract me, the ache tore wide open.

I cried until I couldn't breathe, until the pillow was damp beneath my cheek. The longing for her was unbearable, the ache that reached my bones. That night, all I could think about was how wrong it felt that I could throw her a birthday party without her. That I could tuck myself into bed on the day she was born and not be able to kiss her goodnight. The emptiness swallowed me whole, and I let the tears come because they were all I had left to give her.

In the days that followed, there was a strange stillness, a heavy calm. We had poured so much of ourselves into her birthday that all we could do afterward was sit with the silence. March was nearly over, but the grief was not.

For me, March 17th will always be more than a date. It will always be the day I brought my baby girl into this world. The weight of her in my arms, her first cries, her tiny fingers gripping mine. All of that lives inside me as vividly as if it had just happened. To now live that same date without her, to face her absence instead of her presence, is a wound that will never fully heal.

10

The Blow I Never Saw Coming

I've never owned a pair of rose-colored glasses. My upbringing was a bit harder than most, and I learned at an early age that I was going to have to fight my way through life.

My mother was a drug addict, and the drugs had a stronger grip on her than I ever did. She wanted them more than she wanted me, my siblings, or even my dad. By the time I turned five, she was gone, and custody fell to my father. I wish I could say that brought healing, that his love filled the hole she left behind. But it didn't.

He remarried, and the woman he chose was not a mother to me; she was a wound that kept reopening. My stepmother's words and actions cut deep; she was harsh and unkind. The house we lived in didn't feel like a home. It felt like walking on broken glass, every day measuring my steps to avoid another blow. Whether my dad saw it or chose not to see it, I'll never know. I think he had the potential to be a good father, but in siding with her, in working and being gone, in letting her shape the house, that potential never became my reality.

So I learned to stay small. To read the room before I entered it. To survive in a place where love felt conditional, where safety was always out of reach. By the time I was eight, we were living in a trailer park. Life there was stripped down to the bare minimum. Enough to get by, never enough to feel full. I could see even as a child that we weren't thriving; we were just surviving.

At fifteen, I started working, and the paychecks didn't build me a future; they bought me clothes, gas, and hours away from home. Still, even that small independence mattered. It was a way to breathe. That rhythm carried me until, at seventeen, I became pregnant with Taylor. At eighteen, I was kicked out altogether. By then, struggle felt stitched into every part of me. Survival, loss, starting over, it was the only pattern I knew.

One of the first holes in my story had already been carved years earlier. My mother had been gone since I was five. I saw her only a handful of times after that, but even those visits were marked by the haze of her addiction. Her memory was so far gone that sometimes she didn't even recognize me. Eventually, the visits stopped, and by the time I was a teenager, I had long since stopped expecting her to come back.

So when I learned that she had wandered from a group home, I hadn't laid eyes on her in at least ten years. In 2018, she was officially declared missing by her family. But the truth was, she had been "missing" from my life since I was five years old. I won't say I never thought about her, but thoughts of her were more like passing shadows, not part of my everyday life. I had long since stopped expecting her to realize her wrongs and apologize. It wasn't until years later, around 2021, that my brother, who had become a police officer in the same area where she was last reported missing, decided he needed answers. Something in him just had to know. His search led to the idea of submitting DNA. He did, and that simple cheek swab and test tube eventually unlocked the truth.

In 2022, authorities confirmed through DNA that the partial remains found years earlier in Alabama belonged to her. The match was enough to confirm that the life she once lived was gone, and that her story had ended fatally. It wasn't all of her remains, but it was enough to know.

And so, in January 2023, she was declared legally dead.

My mother's life ended in shadows. She never overcame the grip of addiction. She never came back for us. She never got to know her grandchildren. And when she died, it was pieced together not by family reunions or heartfelt goodbyes, but by bones and DNA reports.

For me, that was the final confirmation of something I had carried all along; she had been gone long before the paperwork ever said so.

I don't think she ever owned rose-colored glasses either. But the difference between her and me would always be this: what I would do for my kids.

So there I was, eighteen years old, kicked out of the house with a newborn and nowhere to go. I was still close to my sister at the time, and though it wasn't some perfector permanent solution, it was a door open to me. That opportunity meant a roof over my head and a place to catch my breath, so I moved in with her and tried to piece together the next step. I grabbed up as many college scholarships and loans as I could, applied for every grant I found online, and worked my butt off as a waitress. I started college eight weeks after Taylor was born at Mississippi Gulf Coast Community College. I took classes during the day and waited all night long. Gratefully, the college had daycare for $900 a semester. I used some of my student scholarship and loan money to pay for daycare and did my best. It was survival, not balance.

But realistically, I was treading water for two and barely making ends meet. But I did everything I could for my baby girl.

I didn't have much direction in life back then, other than what had to get done that day and maybe, if I was lucky, the next day. My mother had dropped out of school in eighth grade, and even though my dad was a military man, I wasn't given a career path or talked to about what I wanted to be when I grew up. I had to blaze my own trail.

It took me eight years to get through college, but I kept at it. Taylor wasn't much older than a year when I met Aubreigh's father. Our romance was short, not because I didn't want stability, but because I quickly learned who he really was. Behind the surface, there were things I could not live with, choices and behaviors that made it impossible to build a safe life together. By then, I already knew how to take care of myself, and I chose to walk away.

Pregnant and unsure of what came next, I spent months trying to figure out where I could build a safe life for Taylor, the baby I was carrying, and myself. I didn't know how it would work out, but I trusted that somehow it would. In the middle of that pregnancy, a door opened. I could move into my own home. It was a massive blessing. Everything had felt like it was falling apart, and I was struggling so hard, a single mom and pregnant, but by the grace of God, I found a tiny house I could move Taylor, Aubreigh, and me into for $750 a month. It was small and perfect for us.

Not long after, my brother, who had also been kicked out of our father's home, moved in with me. It was a blessing. He was working toward his GED, and he helped me with the girls when he could, so I could work and take college courses. For a few years, we leaned on each other, piecing together something that almost felt like stability. When he moved out, I knew I had to make a massive adjustment in life. At the rate I was going, I would never finish college!

Growing up without a mom, unprotected, and with very little may be a character-builder for some people, but for me, it was my armor in life.

Growing up poor was a testament to survival in a world that often pretends you don't exist.

It was a testament to learning how to be creative out of necessity.

It was a testament to carrying invisible weights while still showing up.

It was a testament to making impossible choices and living with their echoes.

Most of all, it was a testament of how much I could love and protect my children with so little remaining for myself.

I always had a huge amount of love to give out. I didn't know I was worthy of unconditional love until much later in life, but I knew how to love my children.

I wanted my babies to feel all the things I didn't know growing up. I wanted them to have everything I could give them. They would always feel loved, cared for, and supported in a way I never did.

My mom chose drugs when I was five. I chose to send my daughter to what I thought was a top school district when Taylor was five.

I had an aha-moment.

I needed to set her up for success with the best education possible. Aubreigh would follow in her footsteps. With the best education possible, I knew they would excel in life. I envisioned the girls with scholarships, full-rides wherever they wanted to go. No college debt. No working nights to pay off loans. They were going to have everything I didn't have, and that was going to start as soon as Taylor stepped foot into a kindergarten classroom.

I looked around Mississippi for the best school district in the state and found Ocean Springs, about 30 miles down the road from where we were living at the time. They were the top-rated school district for academics.

I was enrolled in the nursing program, but beyond burned out. I was up until 1:00 a.m. doing school work and just couldn't do it anymore. I only had a year of school left, but I knew I couldn't keep up that demanding schedule and be a good mom, so I withdrew from the nursing program and transferred into the elementary education program.

I transferred to Southern Mississippi and finally declared my major as elementary education. It took me two more years to finish school, a total of eight years, but I did it. I was the first person in my family to graduate from college. And I knew if I could do it, my children could too.

I got hired right away, but my first year of teaching was in a different district. That same year was Aubreigh's first year of kindergarten and Taylor's first year of second grade, but I wasn't at their school. I knew I needed to gain experience, so I committed to that first year. When it ended, I immediately began applying in ██████████████ so I could be closer to them and create more stability for our family. I was blessed to be offered a position there, and that became the school where both Aubreigh and Taylor attended and where I worked until Aubreigh's passing. I still had mounds of debt to pay off. I worked as a waitress during the summer and even offered tutoring sessions for additional income so I could buy the girls back-to-school clothes and everyday necessities. It was very common for me to have two or three jobs at any given time. But I did what I could to ensure we had enough money for vacations, new clothes, and exciting life experiences. When I got pregnant with Ryker in 2017, his dad and I had already built years of history together. By then, we both understood that while we cared deeply for each other, we were better as friends than as life partners. That realization didn't come with bitterness; it came with peace. Co-parenting with him was a far different experience than what I had known before, and for that, I will always be grateful.

After Ryker, I knew I was done having children. With Ryker, my family felt complete. I had my happy little four, and in so many ways, my heart was full. Life wasn't perfect, but it was ours, and it was good, until it wasn't.

When Aubreigh passed, my world split wide open. My child's death broke me in ways words can never truly hold.

I thought I had already weathered the worst life could hand me. I thought nothing could level me more than burying my child. But life has a way of reminding you it can always cut deeper. I never expected the curveball that came in April 2024. That month, it felt as if the ground gave way beneath me all over again, even after everything I had already endured.

It was Friday, April 19th, 2024.

I was sitting on my couch and got a text from a friend.

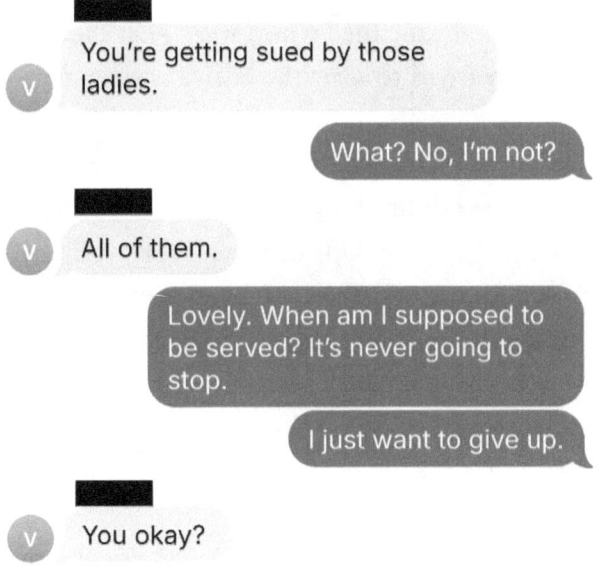

Through my text conversation with my friend, I went for a ride on the small town gossip merry-go-round. It went something like this...

A friend of my friend worked at a local business that offered notary services.

And she personally notarized a one-hundred-seventy-five-page lawsuit against me and Taylor.

And the people filing that weapon against the two of us were the eight parents, representing four of the very children who had tormented my daughter to death.

My friend's friend watched these eight adults laugh and cheer while she did her job.

And the second they left the store, she called my friend to pass it on to me to give me a heads up that I was going to get served.

The cruelty of it all stung just as much as the legal blow.

And I felt like a drowning woman clawing for a lifeline.

As soon as I got off the phone with my friend, I called every attorney in town, leaving messages on every machine. It was a Friday and nobody was at work. I explained who I was, what I learned, and asked for help. And then I had to wait the entire weekend to see if I'd get served.

Those next few days dragged on. I knew a stranger would show up on my doorstep, but I didn't know why or with what.

Come Monday, I got the kids out the door even earlier than normal, went to work, and did the best job I could with only half my mind really at the office. The other half was floating around outside my head, trying to come up with a reason I'd be getting sued.

That night, a man knocked on the door. He didn't look at the camera, he didn't speak into the camera, he just kept knocking. I didn't answer.

On Tuesday, he came back around 4:00 p.m. and did the same thing. But that time, he left a letter on my front door with a phone number to call. That afternoon, I contacted an attorney and was advised to make the call and answer the door the next time the man shows up.

As soon as I hung up the phone with the attorney, I called the number on the letter and learned that, in fact, we were getting served, and the man who had been at my house twice had to serve Taylor personally as well.

"Well, she's a minor, so I'll take anything you have to give her," I insisted.

"No, ma'am. I'm given strict orders that this must also be placed in your daughter's hands," he said.

"There's no way I'm having her deal with this. She's 15 years old."

We went round and round a few times before I finally said.

"Fine."

He was doing his job. And I felt like I failed at mine right then.

The next day, Taylor came home from school around 4:00 p.m., while I was already home with Ryker. It wasn't more than 15 minutes later before there was a knock at the front door. Taylor and I looked at each other and walked to the door side-by-side without saying a word.

"Heather Wyatt," the man asked when I opened the door.

"Yes, that's me," I said, holding out my hand.

He placed a very thick envelope in my hand and then turned to Taylor.

"Taylor Wyatt?" he asked my daughter.

"Yes, sir, that's me," she said and followed my lead by holding out her hand, never breaking eye contact.

He placed a very thick envelope in her hand as well.

We walked inside, shut the door, and opened our packets. That's when we learned that my voice and my daughter's voice had been temporarily stripped away.

The lawsuit those eight parents filed was an emergency order. The judge granted their request without my knowledge, Taylor's knowledge, or anyone from our side even being in the room. The judge signed an ex parte order, sealed the case, and issued an emergency injunction temporarily suspending our social media accounts.

It felt like we were being *served* like criminals. The families had gotten exactly what they wanted and were even bragging about it.

We felt ambushed, which, I guess, is what successful lawsuits do to people. If they were celebrating as it was being notarized, I wondered what they were doing after the judge temporarily suspended my voice.

Did they celebrate?

Did they hug one another?

Did they go home and make promises to their daughters who bullied mine?

I wondered if they knew how devastated we felt. They wanted to prevent us from continuing to share the truths of what Aubreigh endured. That was loud and clear.

For months after her death, I had been publicly raising awareness about bullying and the systems that fail kids like Aubreigh. On social media, I had shared our story, screenshots of the messages Aubreigh received (with the names marked out), posts about what she'd been through, and videos to show other parents that this could happen to any family. It wasn't about revenge. To show others the grief. It was about bringing light to something ugly and hidden, making sure her story could help someone else.

Behind the scenes, though, the backlash grew. Families of some of the same children who had hurt Aubreigh were the ones who had been calling the school district when I worked there, contacting my job, and feeding information wherever they could to discredit me. They worked quietly, but their intent was obvious: silence us.

I was used to disappointment, though. I was so hurt that Taylor was wrapped up in this mess, too. I hated that they were still trying to make Aubreigh into a liar, and I hated that it was happening to Taylor, too.

The worst part about it was that Taylor and I never publicly said any of their names out loud. Ever. Yet we were banished from all social media platforms because I was fighting for my daughter's justice, fighting to bring awareness, fighting to break the stigma introduced me to a new level of trauma, corruption, and rage.

I had grown up poor, clawed my way through life, but that was a new kind of cruelty, one that stole my faith in people, which had cracked further.

Scrambling for Help

The moment I knew, I started desperately calling around, trying to find an attorney. My current lawyer, the one who had been handling some of my social media and advocacy issues, told me he couldn't take this kind of case. He explained this was a chancery matter, and that wasn't his area. I felt like I was drowning while dialing number after number.

Finally, after days of calling and searching, I found someone who would take it on. At first, he seemed like exactly what I needed: proactive, passionate, eager to push this as a First Amendment violation and fight it all the way up if he had to. For the first time since the papers had been shoved into my hands, I felt hope.

But in the meantime, Taylor and I were forced to deactivate our accounts while my attorney tried to work it out. It wasn't just about losing a platform; it was about being silenced. After losing Aubreigh to the torment of bullying, I couldn't believe the bullies' families had found yet another way to target our family. I just wanted to scream! Hadn't they taken enough? I was being muzzled, cut off from the one place I had been able to share Aubreigh's story, to fight for awareness, to try to help others, and to connect with people who reminded me I wasn't alone.

A Heavy Double Standard

Behind the scenes, conversations were happening between the judge and the two attorneys, conversations I wasn't privy to, deals being discussed without me in the room. I pushed and pushed, insisting this was a violation of our rights. Meanwhile, the very children whose parents filed this case stayed on social media. Their attorneys argued that their kids were being threatened, and blamed Taylor and me for it, and yet did nothing to pull their own kids offline.

So my 15-year-old daughter had to listen to lawyers argue that it was *her fault*. My heart continued to get torn into smaller and smaller pieces as I watched her try to process everything in those meetings. In the back of my mind, I had question after question and no answers.

How do I help her now when she's still grieving her sister?

How do I tell her life isn't always this bad, and she won't always get punished for doing the right thing while those who caused harm are protected?

How do I help her cope with this?

I couldn't. I was livid. Our voices were silenced, but the ones who hurt my daughter and Taylor's sister were free to live their lives uninterrupted. We were being told that it's okay for those girls and those parents to tell their version of what happened, but I needed to be silent, and Taylor couldn't share her sister's story. It was a twisted version of justice that left me sick to my stomach.

It was a double standard so sharp it cut to the bone. They could claim victimhood while still keeping their children active online. Meanwhile, we, those who had lost everything, were forced into silence.

April crawled by. Not with big events or milestones, but with the slow ache of waiting. We stayed off social media, our circle pulled tight, life carried out in hushed routines. I spent hours in lawyers' offices, papers stacked in front of me, discussing options, and trying to determine our next steps, bills piling up, each meeting ending with more questions than answers. The weight of legal costs pressed against the weight of grief, as if I didn't already have enough crushing me. Still, it felt like what I had to do, like working and doing everything I could behind the scenes was the only way to keep pushing for Aubreigh's voice to be heard, and now to fight for mine and Taylor's rights to speak.

At home, life carried on in its rhythms. The kids went to school, I worked, and we counted down the weeks until summer break. Yet even in that ordinary routine, the absence was sharp. Every day carried a reminder that she wasn't here to share in it, whether it was a school event she should have attended or the chatter in the carpool line where her voice should have joined in. The constant awareness that our family of four was now three.

So much of April looked like life continuing as normally as possible on the outside. That's what April was, living in two realities at once. The outside world saw a family continuing on. But inside, we were navigating grief, silencing orders, mounting costs, and a legal system that seemed stacked against us. It wasn't just another problem. It was proof that I never seemed to get a break, that just when I thought I'd found my footing, the ground split open beneath me again.

May arrived, bringing another milestone that I knew would drop me to my knees.

Mother's Day arrived with a heaviness I can hardly describe. It was my first without Aubreigh, and even before I opened my eyes that morning, its weight sat on my chest. The calendar, the commercials, the store aisles lined with flowers and cards everywhere I turned, the world seemed determined to remind me of what I no longer had. In years past, she had always gone out of her way to make the day special. Even when she was really little, she would try to cook breakfast for me, toast that was sometimes a little burnt, scrambled eggs a little runny, or just something silly she'd throw together with such pride. She would bustle around the kitchen, determined to surprise me, her smile wide as if serving me a five-star meal.

She wasn't just about the food. She was my empathetic, nurturing child who always tried to make everything perfect for everyone else. On Mother's Day, that meant making sure the house was spotless, straightening pillows, picking up toys, and wiping down the counters. She wanted everything flawless so that I could just rest and feel celebrated. And it always worked, not because of how it looked, but because of the love behind it.

Taylor and Ryker were so sweet. They tried to make the day memorable in their own ways. As thoughtful as always, Taylor tried to take charge, ensuring I didn't have to do too much. With his tender heart, Ryker wrapped his little arms around me and told me, "Happy Mother's Day, Mommy," in the most innocent, matter-of-fact way as though love could fix everything. And in a way, it did help. Their presence, their love, grounded me. They reminded me I was still needed.

But underneath all of it, the ache never stopped because one child was missing. The one who should have been there to hand me a card scrawled in her handwriting, or flowers picked from the yard, or just one of her tight hugs. I thought of years past when she would make me laugh with some silly gift or tease me about being "the best mom ever" in that sarcastic, playful way she had. This year, all I had were memories.

I tried to smile for Taylor and Ryker. I wanted to let them see gratitude in me because they deserved that. But when they weren't looking, tears slipped down my face. I kept thinking, *this is not how it was supposed to be.* A mother's day with one less child isn't really Mother's Day at all. It's survival.

There are no words big enough for the way that day felt. Everywhere I turned, I was reminded of what was missing. Mother's Day cards, flowers in the stores, and social media are filled with smiling children hugging their moms. I celebrated quietly with Taylor and Ryker, grateful for them, but my heart ached with the emptiness of the one who wasn't there. It was a wound that no brunch or bouquet could cover.

Mother's Day came and went, leaving me both grateful and gutted. I was grateful for Taylor and Ryker and for the ways they tried to fill the day with love, but I was gutted for the one who was missing. And before I could catch my breath from that milestone, another one loomed at the end of the school year.

By the end of May, the house was full of end-of-school-year chatter: class parties, yearbooks, awards, and kids counting down the days until summer. I went through the motions with Taylor and Ryker, proud of all they had accomplished, smiling for pictures, and talking about summer plans. But underneath, there was another ache because this should have been a milestone for Aubreigh, too.

It would have been her closing middle school and stepping into high school. She would have been picking out her courses, talking about electives, maybe dreaming about sports or clubs. I could almost hear her excitement, how she would have been buzzing with nervous energy about starting fresh in a new building.

And the following school year would have been the year she and Taylor finally got back in school together. High school. Both of my girls under the same roof again, crossing paths in the hallways, Taylor looking out for her little sister. That's something I had looked forward to for years, imagining them walking in together on the first day, laughing and rolling their eyes at each other, but secretly happy to share that time.

Instead, the school year ended with a hollow space that no awards ceremony, no summer plans could fill. The report cards, the chatter about next year, the excitement of moving up, all shadowed by the reminder of what should have been. Another ending without her. Another season that marked not only time passing, but the future she had been robbed of.

11

May 13th, 2024—Conditional Freedom

From May 13th onward, I was checking in constantly with my attorney via text. Every day felt like it might be the day the judge finally made a decision.

"Do you think it will be today? Will it be a final order or temporary?"

"It'll be temporary," he told me.

"Thank you," I said.

"The final order will come after a hearing."

The day dragged by, and I checked my phone every few minutes. Nothing came in by the time I went to bed.

I woke up on May 14th and grabbed my phone, hoping for an update. But I didn't see anything. I texted my attorney in frustration even before coffee: *Every day that passes is a continued violation. My child is gone. She's the one who is deceased, and yet they still control my life and my surviving daughter's life, while their lives remain unchanged.*

I checked in again on May 15th.

Again, on May 17th.

Again, on May 20th. Still nothing.

On May 21st, my attorney finally had a long call with the judge and the other lawyer, combing through case notes. On May 22nd, he told me they were still bouncing a draft order around, and promised we'd touch base the next morning to hammer out the last issues.

It was like living in purgatory; every sunrise came with the hope of freedom, every sunset ended with disappointment.

Finally, on May 24th. The judge signed the order. Not a final order, but a temporary one, with suffocating stipulations.

I wasn't free. I was shackled.

I listened as the list was read out, each condition weighing heavier on me than the last.

Yes, I could post again and share updates, pictures, and stories. But there was a catch: I was now responsible for monitoring every comment and share across hundreds of thousands of followers.

The task was impossible from the start. I was ordered to delete anything that mentioned the names of the girls who had bullied Aubreigh, or anything that might "harm" them. The expectation was that I'd spend my days glued to a screen, scrolling endlessly, consumed with trying to shield them, hoping I could catch things before anyone else did. If something slipped through, their names or insinuations appeared and were seen, it would immediately be sent to their attorney as evidence that I wasn't following the rules. In other words, I would look like the one at fault.

So instead of returning to social media with relief, I returned in shackles. Every post, update, and comment section became a minefield. I had to comb through thousands of comments, hunting for names, nicknames, and even veiled references. I set up filters, scrolled endlessly, and tried to anticipate the comments before they appeared. But the truth was, no matter how much I monitored, it would never be enough.

And the cruel irony gnawed at me all the while: I wasn't being asked to protect my daughter's name. I was being forced to defend theirs.

To sit there and watch her bullies' names appear, to read insinuations that carried the weight of everything they had done, and then to delete them, it was a wound reopening over and over again. My fingers hit "remove," but my heart screamed, *Why am I the one doing this? Why is my daughter still being silenced, while they are the ones being shielded?*

Somewhere in me, a line began to form, a growing awareness that my energy did not belong to protecting them.

It belonged to protecting her.

That was my "freedom." Conditional. Suffocating.

I did what I was ordered to do through tears, physical pain, and absolute rage, unlike anything else I'd ever experienced.

I was already working full-time, already raising my children, already trying to crawl through grief that consumed me, and now I had to police the internet for the sake of people who had tormented us. It was insulting, humiliating, and impossible.

Why couldn't the judge simply tell those parents to remove their children from social media if they were so concerned?

Why was I, the grieving mother, tasked with protecting them?

Why was I suddenly expected to act as a filter for their reputations?

Why couldn't they remove their children from social media while the adults sorted this out?

Why was I, the victim's mother, carrying this burden?

It felt like yet another violation layered on top of everything else.

Regardless, I conceded. You can't really say no to a judge. So I monitored them as best as possible while receiving daily emails and texts from my attorney about their complaints. They assumed every video was towards them; they assumed every comment was towards them. I knew this was an effort to harass and torment me legally. To try to get me off social media. I refused to let them, though. So as the weeks continued, I maintained a level head, went to work, raised my children, grieved Aubreigh, went to therapy, and did everything I needed to continue forward.

By the end of May, the calendar had inched forward, but the ache hadn't shifted. We had survived holidays, job changes, birthdays, court and legalities, and Mother's Day, and we were still standing. But we were tired, so tired. And I knew, deep down, that this fight, both with grief and with the system that failed my daughter, had only just begun.

12

June 2024—A Mother's Breaking Point

Through June, the back-and-forth with attorneys only escalated. Their lawyers sent lists of demands; I pushed back. Each refusal was met with the same threat: *We'll sue for slander. We'll sue for defamation.* My attorney called me repeatedly with updates, each one another reminder that the families weren't interested in peace. They wanted me silenced.

And yet, while those threats mounted, another decision was unfolding in my personal life. After many tears, prayers, and decision-making, the lease on my current home was up. So much of me wanted to stay. And my landlord was kind and understanding and willing to work with me if I wanted to sign another lease. We could have stayed.

But when I looked around at the reality of where I was emotionally, I realized I wasn't healing there. I was trapped. Every room, every hallway, every quiet night in that house held me in mourning and darkness. It wasn't letting me breathe.

Even before Aubreigh passed away, I had been casually looking at homes. Nothing ever felt right. Nothing ever came through. And after she was gone, I had started looking half-heartedly at rentals here and there, just knowing my lease would eventually run out. Most of the places I saw didn't work out either.

Then one day, a fantastic house popped up online in the neighborhood beside mine, literally only two minutes away. The price was right, almost too reasonable to believe. I wasn't hopeful, but I went to see it anyway. The moment I walked in, something in me shifted. It was light, open, and peaceful. And in one of the rooms, there was a butterfly ceiling fan, like a little sign from her, a whisper that this place was meant for us.

It felt like everything finally fell into place. I hadn't been able to find healing in the old house, but here, I could feel the possibility of it. Moving didn't mean leaving Aubreigh behind. It meant giving myself and my family the chance to carry her forward with us, into a space not suffocated by sorrow but open to light and love. On June 11th, I submitted my application. That same day, the owner told me that if I could move in by June 15th, the house was mine. Within five days of finding it, I was moving in. It felt like fate, like a blessing, like God had dropped it into my lap. It all worked out so beautifully... until the reality of moving in began.

Gradually, I moved us into our new home. I allowed myself to take the time I needed to slowly move each room of the current house into the new house, knowing that the last room I had to pack up and move was Aubreigh's.

But before I could face that, another storm was brewing. Even as I carried boxes into the new house and tried to steady myself, the legal battles only grew louder.

A phone call from my attorney told me plainly: threats of defamation and slander weren't empty words anymore. I wouldn't bow down to their demands, so they were preparing to act. It wasn't just talk anymore. He explained that it was not the type of case he would take, and that if I wanted to fight it, it would cost more than I could imagine. The weight of those words sank in. I realized I had no way forward. No money. No protection. No voice and no way to fight back, unless I found help.

On June 20th, in sheer desperation, I sat down, broken and exhausted, and I opened a GoFundMe. That was the day I admitted to myself, and to the world, that I couldn't do this alone. I went on social media and I put out a simple, vulnerable video.

I told what I could, as best I could, without violating the order: I was exhausted, my children were exhausted, I had no money left, and I was now in need of a third attorney. A third. I said what I could: that I was doing everything possible to give my children a good life, to keep them in therapy, to keep them moving forward, but that I was drowning.

I asked for two things: if anyone knew attorneys who could help, please send me their names. And if anyone could give even a small amount to the GoFundMe, it might be enough to help me survive the next battle.

I pleaded with the people who had supported us all along: *Please, if you can, donate to the GoFundMe. Help us keep fighting.*

The video went out, and the response was immediate and over-whelming. Donations poured in, messages flooded my phone, and strangers offered names of attorneys and words of support I could scarcely hold. Even as the wave of kindness rolled over us, life didn't pause: I still went to work, I still called attorneys, I still fielded emails and phone calls, and I still packed boxes. I kept chipping away at each room, slowly, carefully, saving Aubreigh's room for last.

Her room was the final door I had to open, and on June 26th, when I finally stepped inside what she left behind, so much changed.

I wanted to remember Aubreigh's room the way it was. Her space felt sacred, frozen in time. I set up a camera, determined to record every detail: her bed, her dresser, the posters on her wall. I wanted to remember everything, because once I packed it away, that chapter of our life was gone. All her little treasures would never be placed down by her again. I could never replace any of it. And seeing her in her bedroom was about to be nothing more than memories in a camera.

I took my time as I sorted through her things. I smelled her clothes. I gently ran her bracelets through my hands. I looked through her drawers for trinkets and smiled at the thought of her doing the same thing.

It wasn't easy, but I couldn't rush through it. I wouldn't. I wanted to honor her in her room one final time as I folded her things into boxes and bags.

I finally got to her closet. I started pulling things down from the top shelves and was surprised when I came across an old shoebox. I opened it and wasn't surprised to see that it was a makeshift memory box. I choked back tears at the thought of my sweet baby girl hiding away these little tokens of her childhood.

At first, it was sweet. And I actually felt a little sliver of happiness remembering her going to an old movie, as I rubbed an old movie ticket between my fingers. I laughed at a wrinkled-up candy wrapper and wondered why she'd keep something like that. I pictured her with a group of her friends and wondered if she had a secret crush once upon a time, I never knew about. My heart dropped looking at old pictures with friends, and pins from baseball and football games. She had a little secret treasure box, and I loved that about her.

As I continued to go through each thing and got deeper into the box, I couldn't hold back the tears. It all came rushing back to me and left me sobbing on the floor. Wailing like it was September 2023 all over again.

Oh, Aubreigh.

No.

Baby girl. I'm so sorry.

Tears streamed down my face. I kept rubbing my eyes, hoping they'd stop because I wanted to see what else my daughter kept locked away in her little box. I knew I wasn't going to be able to get through packing up her room without breaking down. The silver lining was that it didn't come until I was almost finished.

I gave myself a brief break, collected myself, and took a deep breath in and out. I swallowed hard and looked down at the box in front of me, and noticed something I hadn't seen through the streams of tears.

Tucked beneath the old photos, candy wrappers, and pins from games, she had a few white envelopes. Almost hidden. My body knew immediately what they were. My chest collapsed. My breath got stuck in my throat, and my gut felt like it was being ripped out from inside me.

And then my mind caught up. There they were.

Her goodbye letters.

I picked up the first envelope. *Mom* she wrote in the center in her sweet handwriting.

"No, no, no!" I screamed as I read the first few words.

"No, no, no," I wailed over and over, as though the force of my voice could undo what my eyes were seeing.

It was suffocating. Crushing. I kept screaming. I screamed until my throat burned.

"No, no, no, no, no!"

I collapsed over the box and felt the weight of all of it pushing down on me. The worst part was that I was there alone. Taylor and Ryker were in our new home. I didn't want them with me as I packed up Aubreigh's room. But after finding the letters, I needed my family.

I had been recording the whole thing. I hit the stop button and first called my brother, barely able to form words.

Gratefully, he was already on the way and arrived quickly. I hung up and called Taylor, my words spilling out as sobs, every breath another scream.

How many screams and tears could that room hold?

There I was again, screaming to God, wracked in unbearable pain, begging my life to be different.

"No, God, please. No. Wake me up from this nightmare, please. Please let this not be my life. Please bring her back!" I yelled.

My heart broke all over again. Seeing Aubreigh's words on paper, acknowledging that she knew we would be devastated without her. Still, she couldn't continue living life anymore, which ripped me apart in a different way than finding her in September.

It felt like the air itself was trembling, like the ceiling might cave under the weight of my sorrow. The room pulsed with sound, each scream bouncing off the walls until it felt as if the house itself was wailing alongside me. Every tear that hit the floor felt heavier than the last, soaking into the tile, as though the room was drowning with me in an ocean of grief.

It felt endless, as though the drywall and floor themselves were absorbing my grief, soaked with a mother's wail. I pushed myself off the ground and started making my way out of her closet, but dropped to my knees, clutching the notes to my chest, my body convulsing, the world around me collapsing.

How many screams could these walls hold?

How many tears could this single room contain?

How can someone's heart and soul shatter so completely and yet their body still go on breathing?

Those questions echoed inside my mind until my brother and Taylor arrived. I had Ryker go over to his dad's house for a while.

When they arrived, we sat together and read the notes, the words my baby had left behind, sobbing and shaking. There are no words in any language for that kind of pain, just guttural cries, only sounds that tear out of you like an animal caught in a trap.

Afterward, I was numb. There was not much I could do after that moment. Thankfully, Nick showed up and helped my brother just pick up where my strength gave out. I cried and watched Nick and my brother quietly put the last of Aubreigh's belongings into the cars to take to the new house or to the storage unit. All that was left was her vanity. Looking at it ignited a rage I didn't know was inside me.

"Burn it," I told my brother. "Burn it to the ground."

My grief had nowhere else to go. I began punching the walls, then the windows, my fists slamming against glass and drywall as anger and despair poured out in waves. My brother wrapped his arms around me from behind, holding me tight as I buckled under the weight of it all.

He kept whispering, "It's going to be okay. It's going to be okay," even though we both knew nothing would ever truly be okay again.

I sank to the floor, gasping through tears. He urged me to leave, telling me, "Go home. Just get out. I'll handle the rest. There are only a few things left to do anyway."

So I went to our new home, without her. I carried the notes with me, and once I was there, I read them repeatedly, searching desperately for some clue, some hidden meaning, anything that might explain why my baby chose this. I just wanted her back.

The house was quiet, but my mind wasn't. I sat surrounded by her words, drowning in them, while at the same time longing to be near her things again. That longing pulled me to the video I had taken earlier, of her room and her belongings, a record of what I could never have again. I pressed play, and in that silent new house, I let the images of her old room wash over me like a ghost of what once was.

And when I got to the part of the video where I realized I was reading her goodbye letters, I got a nudge from the Lord. I knew that I was meant to use my pain for a purpose. I didn't know who would benefit from watching me fall apart on the floor of my deceased daughter's bedroom closet, but I knew I had to trim the video and post it.

I didn't hesitate. I trimmed the video to include the moments of me opening a letter addressed to 'Mom,' and I posted it.

I wanted the world to see what suicide leaves behind. I wanted every teenager to understand that their absence leaves a crater no parent can climb out of. I wanted viewers to see what it does to a family. I wanted other kids to stop, even for one second, and think: I wanted every child who was thinking of giving up to see my face and know: *My mom would care. My dad would care. Someone would be devastated if I left.*

I didn't expect it to go viral, but it did. Millions saw it. Parents and kids alike felt the raw truth of it. Millions wept with me. Parents, grandparents, and Teens who had once felt that same despair or were currently in that despair—it struck them in their bones. For some, it was a lifeline. For others, it was a mirror.

13

The Families Strike Again

I reread Aubreigh's goodbye letters a few hundred times a day over the next handful of days. I could recite them. I memorized them. I hoped that by reading them, over and over again in her tiny handwriting, I could find hints, clues, or something that I hadn't noticed before.

Every chance I got, I'd sneak a look at one of the letters. Taylor read hers. She kept it. We read Rykers to him and put it away for him to have when he's older.

Maybe rereading them would make it easier to cope.

The reality was that nothing would help me in that moment. I was reliving it all again as if it had just happened.

I was a raw nerve. The fact that I was actually breathing, moving, talking, driving, and working was a miracle. And, in the midst of coming to terms with everything, those four families responsible for making my baby question her place on Earth were after me again.

Instead of compassion, instead of any recognition of the

devastation, those four families ran straight back to court claiming that my video of me in Aubreigh's closet was somehow harming their children.

Me. *Me*, as a grieving mother cleaning out my daughter's room, finding goodbye letters from my deceased child, was somehow harmful to their children.

On July 1st, 2024, they requested another emergency injunction and ex parte order.

The court held a telephone conference with the attorneys. Allegations were raised that I had violated the prior order, directly or indirectly. This time, behind closed doors, their attorney, my attorney, and the judge met in chambers after court hours.

The judge pointed to the chaos online from my most recent viral post and said it was creating "complexity." He said that because of the "amount of social media interactions," he agreed with the families and once again signed an emergency order, stripping me of my voice on my social media accounts.

Another gag order. Another muzzle. I was pissed.

When that video went out, it didn't just circulate quietly among a few friends. It exploded. Social media has a way of taking raw truth, especially when it strikes something universal, and turning it into wildfire. That's what happened with me sitting alone in Aubreigh's closet.

People weren't just watching the video; they were responding to it in droves. Comment sections were filled with millions of voices, some offering sympathy, others expressing outrage. Many people said they couldn't stop crying, that they felt as though they had lost a daughter, a sister, or a best friend. My grief became theirs, and the connection was immediate.

On one side, it was sympathetic and heartwarming, with people sharing their own stories of loss, thanking me for speaking out, and promising to hold their children closer. But on the other side, it enraged people. They were furious to learn what Aubreigh had endured and furious at its injustice. To them, it felt personal. It felt like an attack on every child they loved.

That mix of heartbreak and anger made the video spread faster. People shared it not just once but again and again, sending it privately to friends, posting it on their own feeds, stitching it into their own videos with their own words layered on top. Strangers I had never met began retelling my story in their own voices, adding their reactions, their tears, their outrage. The narrative moved beyond me and took on a life of its own.

That's the nature of viral interaction: once it begins, it multiplies exponentially. One person shares, then ten of their friends share, and before long, it's everywhere. In just days, millions of people who had never even heard my name now knew my face, my daughter's name, and her story.

And to the families who raised the girls who bullied my daughter, the support that ran far and wide for me and Aubreigh, somehow hurt them.

And the judge agreed.

And then, as if the floor couldn't fall out from under me any further, my attorney quit right after delivering the news. He left me stranded, silenced, and scrambling again to find someone willing to fight for me.

God, what am I doing wrong?
Am I being punished for something?
Am I in the wrong here?
Is this all my fault?
Should I just stop?
Should I walk away?
Should we move and start over in a new town?

What do I need to do to make this nightmare end?

I was at a loss. My brain ran rampant, chasing itself in circles with doubt and exhaustion. Little did I know that the emergency order fit perfectly into what they had planned for the next day. They wanted me quiet, silenced, stripped of my voice once again, just in time for their next move.

I was exhausted—emotionally, financially, and spiritually. We had just moved, and my bills were piling up. I had already drained resources paying one attorney, and now I needed another. I was still off social media, still locked out of the one place where I could tell my daughter's story, and still fighting uphill against families who seemed determined to break me any way they could.

July 2nd, 2024—Civil Court Filing

The next day, July 2nd, I shuffled into the kitchen, brewed my coffee, and tried to steady myself for another day. The house was quiet, too quiet, but that had become normal by then. I checked my phone per usual. A flood of notifications lit up the screen. Texts. Missed calls. Messages asking the same thing:

"Have you seen the news?"

"Heather, are you okay?"

"What's going on?"

And then I saw it, not from an attorney, a courthouse, or even someone willing to speak to me face-to-face, but in bold black print splashed across the front page of the local newspaper I was holding in my hands. The families filed separate cases in civil court, including slander, libel, and more. It was a copy of the same accusations repackaged in new language. And again, I wasn't served. I found out in the most degrading way possible: reading about myself in the local newspaper.

While that was going on, apparently, the gag order had been leaked. The world was slowly finding out. The news of it all spread like wildfire. People were outraged. Hundreds of videos poured in, calling out the injustice, declaring this a violation of free speech, standing up for me when I couldn't stand up for myself. This resonated so deeply because it wasn't just any video. It was a mother already broken open by the loss of her child, still trying to advocate and share so others might be spared this pain. It was a woman who had been bullied out of her job, then relentlessly targeted by the very families connected to her daughter's suffering, and finally pressed down by the weight of the courts themselves. People saw the layers of cruelty stacked on top of unbearable grief, and they cared. They cared because it was unjust. After all, it could have been their daughter, sister, or family. They cared because love rises louder than cruelty, and they wouldn't let me carry that fight alone.

The Uprising of Support

Something extraordinary began to happen between July 2nd and the court date on July 18th. Strangers, neighbors, and entire communities who had watched the injustice unfold decided they would not sit silently.

Thousands of dollars poured in from people I had never met a few weeks before, from mothers, fathers, grandparents, and students, and each message was tucked with words of encouragement: *We believe you. We're with you. Keep fighting.*

Restaurants across the Gulf Coast painted their windows with Aubreigh's name and messages of solidarity. Some wrote in bold letters: *You can't silence us all.* Others painted butterflies and hearts, symbols of love that now carried her spirit into every street corner. Shirts began to appear too, printed and sold in towns I had never even visited, with slogans like: *We will speak for you* and *We've got your back.*

#LLAW was painted in purple and pink, and the pink colors from The Aubreigh Wyatt Foundation logo lit up school events, grocery store aisles, and baseball fields, reminders that people cared and that our story had reached far beyond the courthouse walls.

Businesses and companies found ways to help in whatever form they could.

- Some set out jars by the registers to raise funds for legal fees.
- Others donated a portion of their sales for the month to support our fight.
- Coffee shops and tea shops created the Aubreigh Wyatt drink.
- Churches opened their doors for prayer vigils.
- Small boutiques sold bracelets etched with her name.

It was as if everyone had decided that if the courts tried to silence me, they would raise their voices louder on my behalf. The world took on Aubreigh as their baby girl, and my heart ached with gratitude.

The response and support for Aubreigh renewed my faith in humanity. It stoked the fire in the pit of my belly that had been dampened by those families for so long. For the first time in years, I felt like we could actually make a difference. My voice might have been muted again, but I saw love everywhere again.

For Aubreigh.

The wave of support grew so massive that it spilled far past Mississippi. Social media posts appeared from Arizona, Alabama, Louisiana, Texas, and beyond. It started to reach into Canada, Europe, Australia, and so much more! People organized community events, candlelight vigils, and fundraisers, sharing pictures of families holding up signs that read: *Justice for Aubreigh*. My phone buzzed endlessly with texts and calls with messages of hope and screenshots of the countless ways people were standing up for us. People were offering to join The Aubreigh Wyatt Foundation board, support us in ways I never saw coming.

It was overwhelming in the best way. In the middle of being stripped down by courts, attacked by families, and left wondering if I could go on, the world answered back with love. The louder they tried to silence me, the louder the community roared. That uprising of support carried me straight into July 18th, when the courthouse itself would tremble with the sound of Aubreigh's name.

They stepped in to carry the message when I couldn't. The world was watching.

On July 16th, I got a phone call from the local newspaper reporter who was writing about my life. She asked me if I wanted to comment on the news that the families withdrew their civil suit. I didn't have a comment. At least, not one I wanted in the paper. I kept my thoughts to myself, said goodbye, and hung up.

Just like that, it was gone. But it didn't matter. The bigger showdown was still coming. My court date was set for July 18th. And I had to get a new attorney before then.

July 18th, 2024—The Courthouse on Lockdown

The morning began quietly enough. I had taken the day off work; court wasn't scheduled until 1 PM, but the day felt loaded with anticipation. I breathed slowly, sipping coffee as the sun rose. The air in the house felt thick, charged with dread and expectation. Even with the hours stretched before me, my nerves were raw from the moment I woke up.

I chose a black professional dress, something strong and respectful, and curled my hair with deliberate precision as if a measured outward appearance could steady the storm inside my chest. Alone in the kitchen, I prayed silently, asking for strength I didn't feel.

Taylor chose not to come; she stayed home. Because of the court's restrictions, the courts had sealed the case, so no one was allowed in the courtroom. She wouldn't be allowed inside. Nick planned to meet me later. My brother Jeff couldn't take off work. So it was me, Dexter, Kelly, and Ryker riding together that morning. I didn't drive myself to the courthouse. I couldn't. My nerves were shot, my mind racing too fast to focus on the road. I was a mess, a nervous wreck, and too anxious to think about navigating traffic.

We knew there would be a crowd waiting, maybe even chaos, and the thought of pulling up alone was unbearable. Sitting beside them in the car gave me something solid to hold on to, a reminder that I wasn't walking this road alone, even in the swirl of nerves and fear.

The drive wasn't long, but the anticipation made every mile feel heavy.

When we pulled up to the courthouse, my heart caught in my throat. This wasn't an ordinary day in Pascagoula. The court building, usually just another brick building on Magnolia Street, looked like it had been transformed into something out of a standoff. Roads around it were blocked. The entire docket for the day had been cleared, and every other case had been canceled except mine. Media there. Snipers stood on the roof. It felt like a war zone.

Yet, what greeted me first wasn't chaos; it was love. A sea of pink stretched along the courthouse edges, people holding signs, wearing shirts honoring my daughter. They weren't there to condemn; they were there to lift. "Justice for Aubreigh," "Let her speak," "We stand with Heather." Strangers shouting her name like a prayer, like a promise. My throat tightened. I whispered, "Thank you, God," feeling surrounded and seen.

When it was time to go inside, Kelly walked beside me, Ryker's stepmom. She stood beside me, steadying me, and walked with me up to the courthouse's front doors. I remember clinging to her presence and how she quietly matched my steps.

At the doors, my attorney was waiting. She greeted me there, and together we crossed the threshold. That was the moment the noise of the outside chanting, the sea of pink, the hum of cameras clicking fell away. Inside, the air was heavy and still, and the reality of what I was walking into pressed in hard.

Through metal detectors, I realized I couldn't bring anything in, not even my purse or phone. I stepped back, calling to Kelly, who rushed over, taking the bag so I could go forward empty-handed. We were led down corridors to separate waiting rooms. The other families were tucked in on the right; I was guided left, along with my attorney: silent walls, hushed voices, the mutter of distant footsteps, heavy police presence.

My heart was pounding in that small conference room in the quiet. As we waited, my attorney whispered beside me, planning and preparing, and there was no way I could calm myself down. My anxiousness pressed against me like a weight. My nerves had me restless, my fingers tapping against the table. My chest was tight, my palms damp.

I tried to breathe evenly and sit still, but I was a mess. My thoughts ran in circles, colliding into each other. Every creak of the floor outside, every muffled voice in the hall made my heart lurch, as if the next moment would decide everything. I knew I had to walk into that courtroom and hold myself upright, but inside, I was unraveling.

When the officer opened the door and motioned for us to enter, my legs felt heavy, like they didn't belong to me. I forced them to move anyway, one foot in front of the other, into the silence of the courtroom.

When the time came, my attorney and I walked into the Court-room. The families and their attorneys entered after us.

The courtroom felt hollow, the benches stripped bare. No friends. No family. It wasn't because they didn't want to be there; it was because they couldn't.

The case was sealed.

Sealed means the doors are shut to everyone. The records, filings, and testimony are locked away from public view as if the case doesn't exist. When a case is sealed, it's only the judge, the attorneys, the par-ties involved, and no one else.

The court justified protecting minors' names and identities because they were connected to the case. On paper, that sounded like protection. It meant I had to sit in that courtroom completely alone. No Taylor, no Nick, no church family, no friends or neighbors who wanted to stand beside me. Just me, my attorney, and across the room, the families with theirs.

Walking into a sealed courtroom feels like stepping into silence. The support is still out there on the streets, in the messages, in the hearts of people standing outside, but once those doors close, it's gone. You're left facing the judge's bench and the weight of the law, without a single familiar face to look to for comfort.

On paper, the idea was shielding children. But in practice, it meant total silence. It meant my voice and the truth of what had happened were buried under legal tape.

That's why the local media attorneys were already there that morning.

"All rise," the bailiff called. We stood as the judge entered, robes sweeping as he sat at the bench.

A single moment, and everything shifted.

Before the judge even addressed the case, they rose and argued. They asked that the case not remain sealed. They said the public had a right to transparency, that this wasn't just about minors, it was about free speech, accountability, and justice.

The judge listened carefully, weighing the request aloud. He explained in detail what "sealed" meant, why it had been put in place, and why he was now agreeing to lift it. The minors' personal information would remain protected, yes. But the broader case, the motions, the orders, the hearings would no longer be locked away. The public had the right to know.

With that, the reporters at the room's edges were allowed to stay. The seal cracked open, and light spilled in. For the first time in weeks, it didn't feel like everything was happening in the shadows.

The order of business had been set, and the ground rules were made clear. The case was no longer hidden. And then, the proceedings began.

The hearing itself was unlike anything I had ever experienced. I had walked into that courtroom expecting some kind of back-and-forth, attorneys making arguments, questions asked, points debated, maybe even the chance for me to speak if it came to that. But it didn't happen that way.

Instead, the judge had already read everything: our filings, their motions, the arguments on paper. And when he came in, he simply delivered his decision. No one spoke, not me, not my attorney, not theirs.

As the judge spoke, I just sat there, hands folded in my lap, hardly daring to move. My attorney sat beside me, quietly scribbling a few notes as if anchoring herself in the flood of words. Across the room, the families sat silent, their attorney still. And off to the side, the court reporter typed steadily, her fingers moving across the machine without pause, capturing every word for the record.

It went on and on, the judge's voice filling the courtroom. I tried to keep up and listen to what each sentence might mean for me, but the words blurred together. They were precise, legal, deliberate, and seemed to stretch forever. I genuinely don't know how long it lasted. Minutes? An hour? Time bent in that moment, dragging itself out like it wanted to make me sit in the weight of it.

I remember glancing once at my attorney's notepad, hoping for some clarity, some sign of what this all meant. But she stayed focused, jotting in quick shorthand. And so I sat in the silence, waiting for the gavel to fall, not knowing whether I was about to walk out more silenced than before, or finally, free.

And then, just like that, it was over. No closing arguments, no back-and-forth, no chance for anyone to speak. The judge had said what he came to say, and the proceeding ended as abruptly as it had begun.

When it was over, the families filed out first, and then their attorneys and I exchanged a brief word at the table. That was it.

I remember sitting there confused, almost frozen. I wasn't sure what had just happened. I hadn't had a single moment to feel joy or relief because I genuinely didn't know what had been decided. Some of me even felt angry, or maybe cheated, like I'd been robbed of my chance to be heard.

Afterward, my attorney and I went back into the conference room, and I looked at her, bewildered, and asked, "What's going on?" My emotions hadn't caught up yet because I had no idea what the ruling meant.

She explained calmly: we didn't have to speak because the judge had already read through everything. He had decided based on the filings alone, and he issued it then and there. The outcome was clear: the gag order was lifted, and my voice was restored. Eight stipulations were attached: no naming the families, no insinuations, no veiled references, careful language meant to protect their identities.

On one hand, it still felt like a violation of my First Amendment rights. I couldn't ignore that reality. Even being "free," I was still told what I could and couldn't say. But on the other hand, it was a step forward, a crack in the cage I had been living in. I was no longer silenced. I was no longer under the gag.

It wasn't complete freedom, but it was enough for me to breathe again, finally.

When I walked out of the courtroom, my attorney beside me, I was relieved but exhausted. The weight of months of silencing, shaming, fighting it all pressed down. And then I heard it.

The crowd erupted in unison. "AUBREIGH! AUBREIGH! AUBREIGH!"

The sound split me open. I crumpled into tears, overwhelmed by the love, the solidarity, the sheer force of people who refused to let cruelty win. All I could do was cry and whisper "Thank you," again and again.

The families had tried to silence me, erase my daughter, and make us villains. But that day, the world spoke louder. Evil tried to quiet us, but love roared back.

EPILOGUE

ONE CHAPTER OF THE BATTLE HAD BEEN FOUGHT, AND FOR the moment, I had won. But I knew in my gut there was more to come. Conversations with attorneys continued behind the scenes, each one reminding me that this fight was far from finished. The families hadn't gone silent, and the legal threats hadn't disappeared.

This was not the end of the war. It was only the close of one round. There was still so much more to fight for, so much more to do.

And yet, even as the legal battles loomed in the background, the world around me kept showing up with love.

Businesses, restaurants, boutiques, and community groups continued to honor her name. Painted windows, jars for donations, shirts, and bracelets appeared everywhere I turned. Every time I walked into a shop or scrolled through social media, I saw her face, her name, her story alive in the hearts of others.

People were still finding ways to raise money, to keep the fight moving, to remind me that we weren't alone. Events in honor of

Aubreigh, in honor of bullying prevention, in honor of mental health and suicide awareness kept appearing on the calendar.

The work was far from finished, and even though the world seemed determined to remind me of that, I also felt very reassured that I was not fighting alone.

Their support reached into every corner of our lives, sometimes through quiet gestures, sometimes through loud, unforgettable moments.

A few nights after the July 18th court date, Taylor and I found ourselves at a Zach Bryan concert. He was a musician Aubreigh adored, the kind of artist she would have begged to see live. We went for her, knowing it was something she would have loved. That night, as the music poured out across the crowd, people came up to us—strangers and friends alike, hugging us, offering words of encouragement, telling us how much they supported us.

Some wanted pictures, some just wanted to share their love. The sheer amount of kindness overwhelmed me. Taylor and I screamed the lyrics, we danced, and we let the music carry us. For a brief moment, it felt like we were living out something Aubreigh would have wanted, celebrating in her name.

The end of July and the beginning of August brought another kind of milestone. One that pierced deeper than I expected. For the first time, both Ryker and Taylor were starting a new school year without their sister. More firsts, when would they stop? I hated how badly each cut open the wound again, reminding me that time wasn't carrying us away from the pain, it was carrying us through it, into new versions of it.

But Ryker started second grade at his new school. He looked so small, so young, his backpack nearly swallowing him. His smile carried strength, the kind of brave smile only a seven-year-old can force when he knows everyone is watching. But I could see it, the way his eyes darted, the way his hand fidgeted at his side, like it was reaching for someone who should have been there to squeeze it. In those morning pictures, the space beside him was louder than anything else, an absence that could never be filled. He was trying to be brave, but bravery at seven years old should mean showing off your new shoes or talking about what's in your lunchbox, not walking into a school year with a piece of your heart missing.

And then Taylor. My strong, beautiful girl, beginning her junior year. This wasn't just her first year without Aubreigh; it would have been the year they were reunited. Taylor as a junior, Aubreigh as a freshman. I could see it so clearly in my mind: the two of them walking the same halls again, arguing over clothes in the morning, rolling their eyes at each other in passing, laughing together at night when the world was finally quiet. Instead, empty of that joy, echoing with what could have been.

Our traditional first-day-back-to-school pictures echoed too, not with laughter and inside jokes, but with silence. Smiles masking heartbreak. Arms not quite sure where to rest, because the arms they wanted to wrap around weren't there anymore.

So Taylor and Ryker stood together outside, holding one of the large canvas pictures of Aubreigh. Two kids, sixteen and seven, trying to honor a sister who should have been there to stand between them. It was their way of including her in the back-to-school tradition she had always been a part of. The picture they took was everything all at once, beautiful and heartbreaking, proud and gutting, strong and shattered.

Watching them pose with her picture broke me in ways I can hardly explain. They were just children, trying to live through a world that had already taken too much from them. And I was their mother, aching because I couldn't protect them from this reality. The photo captured their smiles, but what I saw was the weight in their eyes, the missing, the longing, the love that would never fade but would forever ache.

Our traditional first day pictures back to school pictures echoed with what could have been, what should have been.

Even as we pushed through the heaviness of those school milestones, life kept placing new moments in front of us. Some were painful reminders, others carried unexpected beauty.

Later in August, another event carried us forward: a Bikers Against Bullying rally. The turnout was massive. Rows of motorcycles, vendors, food trucks, and families came together, all in Aubreigh's name. The people were amazing, supportive, kind, and determined to stand against the very thing that had taken her from us. It was one of those moments where I could look around and see, with my own eyes, how deeply her story had moved others.

I arrived early, before the roar of engines filled the air. At first, it was quiet, just me mingling, talking with the organizers, meeting vendors, taking in the sight of people gathering for my girl. She would be so honored. Tables were set up with food, booths lined with bracelets and shirts, and I could already feel the heartbeat of a community coming together.

But nothing prepared me for what happened next. The riders had begun their journey in Pascagoula, and they made sure to drive through Ocean Springs on their way, riding straight through the very town that had held my daughter's life, her laughter, her heartbreak, and her story. They rode for her. They rode to honor her.

And they rode for something bigger, for other kids like her, for the mothers and fathers who carried the same fear and ache I carried. In me, they saw themselves. In Aubreigh, they saw their own children. Some of them may have even seen pieces of who they once were, the younger version of themselves who had felt left out, bullied, unseen. Others saw their own brothers and sisters in her, the sibling they once fought with, laughed with, leaned on, or swore they would protect.

Everyone there, in some way, could envision themselves as Aubreigh, or imagine Aubreigh as their child, their sibling, their loved one. And that's what made it so crushingly beautiful. She wasn't just *my* daughter in that moment. She became *everyone's*. Her story was etched into their hearts, pressing on their own scars, awakening their deepest love and deepest grief all at once.

And then, in one long wave, they began to pull in. Hundreds of motorcycles, one after another, engines rumbling like thunder across the pavement. The sound shook the ground, but what shook me even more was the love behind it. I stood there watching, and I couldn't hold myself together. Tears streamed down my face. I broke. Not from pain this time, but from the overwhelming beauty of it all.

In that moment, my heart and soul felt both shattered and soothed. These men and women, most of whom had never met Aubreigh, showed up for her in the loudest, boldest way possible. It was kindness on wheels, power and gentleness rolled into one. It was beautiful. It was sweet. And it was one of those rare moments in grief where the love of others carried me higher than the weight of my loss. The roar of engines became a chorus of love, each rider declaring with their presence that her life mattered, that her story mattered. Tears poured. It was one of those moments where I could look around and see, with my own eyes, how deeply her story had moved others.

My daughter, my baby girl. I knew she would change the world. I just never knew it would be in this way.

Not too long after that, *People Magazine* released an article titled *Fighting for Aubreigh*. Speaking with them, sharing her story on such a large platform, was both an honor and a privilege. Seeing her name in those pages was proof that her life and her truth mattered, that even the biggest stages were listening.

But even in the middle of that pride, a shadow hung over me. September was coming. My body knew it, my mind knew it. Grief is strange like that. It builds an ache inside you before the calendar ever confirms it. I could feel it in the heaviness of my chest, in the way I caught Taylor staring off in silence, in how Ryker clung a little tighter at night. The closer we drew to September 4th, the more the air seemed to shift. It was an impending doom, a knowing ache that no article, no event, no outpouring of love could soften.

We were finally notified on September 1st. After nearly a year of waiting and weeks of worry, they told us the headstone would be there in time. Relief rushed in, but so did urgency. We had to clear the area so the crews could bring in the cranes, trucks, and heavy machinery it would take to set it. We carefully moved every flower, every decoration, anything that might be in their way, making space for what we had prayed would come.

On September 2nd, the headstone arrived. It took time! Hours of careful lifting and adjusting, before it was placed. By September 3rd, it was set and final. A massive black granite butterfly, five feet tall and four feet wide, with a matching black bench, black ledger, and black vases. It was breathtaking. Bold and beautiful, just like her.

And then came September 4th, 2024. One year.

Her resting place is adorned with light pinks, dark pinks, and white. Roses and carnations. Angel wings cradling a display of flowers. The letter *A* spelled out in blooms. A four-leaf clover made from petals. Bouquets upon bouquets, layered against the black stone. Every color, every flower chosen to surround her in beauty. Against the granite, it was striking, sacred, and unforgettable.

Taylor, Ryker, Kelly, Dexter, Mandy, Bailee, my brother Jeff, and I all gathered together. We brought a tent, blankets, and food, setting up a little picnic beside her grave. We told stories. We giggled at memories. We cried. We sat with her, as if she were still right there with us. The day was soaked in grief, but also in love.

It had been one year since my world had shattered. One year since I lost my baby girl. One year of battles, heartbreak, support, and survival. And as we sat there, I realized that her story had become more than just mine; it belonged to everyone who had been touched by her light.

Aubreigh wasn't forgotten. She never would be.

I'd make sure of that.

ABOUT THE AUTHOR

*H*EATHER WYATT IS A DEVOTED MOTHER, ADVOCATE, AND storyteller whose life was forever changed by the loss of her 13-year-old daughter, Aubreigh, to the devastating effects of bullying and the pressures of social media. Transforming her grief into purpose, Heather founded *The Aubreigh Wyatt Foundation*, dedicated to raising awareness about mental health, bullying prevention, and suicide awareness, while providing resources for families and teens in need.

With an audience of over two million followers across social media, Heather shares raw, unfiltered glimpses into her journey, blending vulnerability, hope, and advocacy to inspire change and remind others they are never alone. Her work has been featured in *People* magazine and across national media platforms, amplifying her mission to give a voice to those who feel unheard.

In her debut book, Heather invites readers into her world with unflinching honesty, offering not only the story of her daughter's vibrant life and the events that led to her passing, but also the lessons of resilience, faith, and love that continue to guide her. She lives in Ocean Springs, Mississippi, with her children, finding strength in her family, her faith, and the enduring belief that even in the darkest moments, light can be found.

www.ingramcontent.com/pod-product-compliance
Lightning Source LLC
Chambersburg PA
CBHW021139130626
46554CB00005B/1576